'The power of this case for "exploratory goal-corrected psychotherapy" (EGCP) lies in the diversity of the issues covered: From the broad sweep of theory – the historical evolution of the understanding of the Transference from Freud via Fairbairn, Guntrip and Neuroscience to Heard and Lake's extension of Bowlby's Attachment Theory – to the tiny minutiae of inter-personal interactions, translating the template of mother-infant videoed observation studies to the adult-to-adult psychotherapy domain, from individual to group therapy, we get an integrated perspective which rings true. In short this is vintage McCluskey.'

—**Dr. Tirril Harris**, Kings College London

'In this original and important work, McCluskey and O'Toole bring insights from Attachment Theory and research and Interpersonal Psychoanalysis to bear on professional care-giving. They show convincingly how tone of voice, prosody, and body posture are preconditions for the goal corrected affect attunement that forms the basis of successful psychotherapies. Their training groups help practitioners to understand their countertransferences, the origins of defensive caregiving, and move towards the joint exploration which is the mutative edge of therapies. An accessible and pragmatic volume with vital messages for all serious care-giving professionals.'

—**Prof. Jeremy Holmes**, University of Exeter

'This new work by Una McCluskey and Michael O'Toole is one of the most encouraging books to emerge in the practice and theory of psychotherapy for a long time. It contains one of the best accounts of a therapeutic relationship in the crisis of reliving and making sense of an original trauma. Stunning, loving and benign. Bravo!'

—**Colin Kirkwood**, Psychoanalytic Psychotherapist, Edinburgh.

GW00776160

Transference and Countertransference from an Attachment Perspective

Locating the phenomenon of transference within an evolutionary perspective, this important book develops a new form of dynamic therapy that focuses on the dynamics of attachment in adult life and will be of use to a range of mental health professionals and those at all levels in the caring and education professions.

Transference and Countertransference from an Attachment Perspective: A Guide for Professional Caregivers explores the ways in which transferential phenomena can be located in the different aspects of the self that are instinctive, goal-corrected, and interrelated. At the centre of the book is the idea that when intrapersonal or interpersonal systems (aspects of the self, such as careseeking, caregiving, sharing interests, sexuality, self-defence, building a home) get aroused, the behaviour that follows is only logically and meaningfully connected when the system (aspect of the self) reaches its goal. Placing this new theoretical and clinical approach within the psychoanalytic tradition, the work of developmental psychologists, and the field of neuroscience, the book takes us to the heart of the clinical encounter and explores a range of issues including trauma, the effect of early misattunements, love and hate in the therapeutic relationship, burnout in caregivers, and the need for exploratory care for caregivers themselves.

Building on the therapeutic modality that emerged from the research described in McCluskey's *To Be Met as a Person* (2005), this book provides a valuable guide for psychologists, psychotherapists, medical practitioners, nurses, social workers, organizational consultants, educators, coaches, and workplace managers.

The McCluskey model for exploring the dynamics of attachment in adult life which underlies the work described in this book is currently being practised in a variety of settings and with different ages and communities. These include end-of-life care, organizations, homelessness, mental health, dementia care, children, adolescents and families, schools, pastoral work, training of clinical psychologists and attachment-based psychoanalytic psychotherapists, occupational therapy, art therapy, private practice, domestic violence, police training, GP support and consultation, nurse training and support, pain management clinics, foster carers, social workers, couple relationships, supervision of psychotherapists and counsellors, therapeutic communities, and complex grief and learning disabilities.

Una McCluskey is an Honorary Research Fellow at the University of York. She is a psychoanalytic psychotherapist, a trainer, consultant, researcher, and supervisor. She developed and rated the concept of 'goal-corrected empathic attunement' (GCEA), a key factor in the therapeutic alliance and essential in regulating both careseeking and fear. She has developed a model of psychotherapeutic practice based on the dynamics of attachment in adult life, called exploratory goal-corrected psychotherapy (EGCP). This model is relevant to individual, group, and organizational development. She has an international reputation in the attachment field and has developed a community of professionals who are trained and experienced in the practice of EGCP. She has published widely in the field.

Michael O'Toole is a Registered Counselling Psychologist and Psychotherapist. Michael works in private practice in the west of Ireland. He has taught and lectured for many years in the University of Limerick and is currently offering the model presented in this book to trainees at the Bowlby Centre in London. He has published papers exploring clinical dilemmas in the field of attachment.

Transference and Countertransference from an Attachment Perspective

A Guide for Professional Caregivers

Una McCluskey and Michael O'Toole

LONDON AND NEW YORK

First published 2020
by Routledge
2 Park Square, Milton Park, Abingdon, Oxon OX14 4RN

and by Routledge
52 Vanderbilt Avenue, New York, NY 10017

Routledge is an imprint of the Taylor & Francis Group, an informa business

British Library Cataloguing in Publication Data
A catalogue record for this book is available from the British Library

Library of Congress Cataloging-in-Publication Data
A catalog record has been requested for this book

ISBN: 9781138347731 (hbk)
ISBN: 9780367340988 (pbk)
ISBN: 9780429323911 (ebk)

Typeset in Times New Roman
by Taylor & Francis Books

This book is dedicated to Dorothy Heard and Brian Lake

Contents

Foreword

This new work by Una McCluskey and Michael O'Toole is one of the most encouraging books to emerge in the practice and theory of psychotherapy for a long time. The world of psychotherapy is full of warring tribes, each seeking to advance their own cause by building protective walls round the territory they claim. It is deeply ironic, indeed tragic, that the capacity to embrace other perspectives and engage in dialogue as a normal method of practice is so often absent. Instead of dialogue there is contempt, disparagement, and the reiteration of one's own superiority.

Several features differentiate McCluskey and O'Toole's approach. First of all, they try to integrate personalist and relational perspectives with behavioural, cognitive, developmental, and neuroscientific research. Second, they start from and return to practice, always allowing clients or patients to speak directly on their own behalf. Client accounts of their understanding of their experiences are not reduced to illustrating the latest captivating theory. Third, our authors treat seriously the idea of the self as relational, and take care to identify distinct aspects of the self. McCluskey calls these basic interpersonal systems 'both autonomous and relational' and explores how they interact with each other.

Before proceeding to consider their conceptualizations of the self, it is worth listing the historical sequence of influences they acknowledge, underlining that these influences are practical, theoretical, and research-based. They include Bowlby, Ainsworth, Heard and Lake, McCluskey herself, Stern, Holmes, Damasio, and other neuroscientific contributors.

The aspects of the self which work together in a restorative process to create as much well-being as possible are our careseeking self; our caregiving self; our defensive self; the self which engages in exploratory interest sharing with peers; our sexual self; the self which seeks to create a supportive external environment; and finally the self which builds up an internal environment consisting of internalized experiences of relations with others over our lifetime, experiences which may be supportive or unsupportive of our self as a whole in its relationships.

To this map of our self in relationships with others are added two distinct new concepts. The first is the notion of a keystone system, which is exercised by 'investing' in any one or more of the above aspects of the self, depending on what support is being sought. The keystone system, the authors argue, is at the centre of personal well-being.

The second is a reimagined understanding of the relational processes of transference and countertransference. Out goes a crude distinction between the real relationship and the transference/countertransference relationship. In comes a more sophisticated understanding based on what support the particular aspect of the self that is currently in the ascendant is seeking from the therapist at this moment. The therapist has to help the client to bring into awareness the emotional effects of events that have happened to them in the past, and elucidate what is being sought in the therapeutic relationship now.

All of this makes good sense to me as a practising therapist, supervisor, and person engaged in a lifelong struggle to understand my own self/other vicissitudes in family, community, culture, society, and world over a long lifetime. It is not the only meaningful language on offer: there are many others. But it contains one of the best accounts of a therapeutic relationship in the crisis of reliving and making sense of an original trauma. Stunning, loving, and benign. Bravo!

Colin Kirkwood
Psychoanalytic psychotherapist, Edinburgh

Acknowledgements

We would like to acknowledge all those who have encouraged and supported us in the writing of this book. We thank Rod Tweedy at Karnac Books who commissioned the book from Una McCluskey in 2014, having noticed that Una was giving workshops on the subject in London and elsewhere. It has undergone many transformations since then, but the main one was asking Michael O'Toole to join her as co-author. With Michael on board the book began to take shape and we have worked, happily, solidly, and companionably on it since.

Una would like to thank her friends, colleagues, and mentors who have inspired, enabled, and supported her over many years. She would particularly like to mention Douglas Haldane, Jock Sutherland, Sula Wolff, Dorothy Heard, Brian Lake, Mary Peacey, Caroline Amory, Sally Wassell, Ann Kutek, Liza Bingley Miller, Celia Downes, Ian Sinclair, Yvonne Agazarian, and Fran Carter.

She thanks all those who have trained with her and taken part in supervision groups, which has allowed the theory and the practice to reach such diverse fields as child development, adult mental health, end of life, homelessness, pastoral work, couple work, dementia, and many others. She thanks Simon Wale, Nodlaig Moore, and Niamh Lynch for taking the group work described in this book to students undertaking their doctorate in clinical psychology. The same thanks go to Joanna Stevens, Michael O'Toole, and Jane Cato who have brought the group experiential work to the Bowlby Centre in London so that those training in attachment-based psychoanalytical psychotherapy can be exposed to this developmental process for themselves.

Thanks also to Eliane Meyer, who has taken the model into the field of further education and who can see its relevance for PhD supervision. Jose Miguez, professor of psychology at the University of Porto, gets a special mention for the continuous work he has done over many years using GCEA as part of the training for psychology students and for the research he has carried out in this field. A great deal of thanks go to Nicola Neath who has taken the work into the field of higher education and has shown its relevance to organizational development and leadership training. Thanks to Jim Gunn who has faithfully transcribed many hundreds of hours of group material, which has enabled a rigorous examination of the group process.

Una owes a particular debt to Sarah Wills, her PA who has ensured that the work explored in this book has survived and thrived due to her enormous capacity to relate directly and warmly to all who have been associated with the work. Thanks to JB who has been there all the time.

Michael would like to thank first and foremost Una McCluskey for inviting me to collaborate on this project. I wish to thank the people in my supervision group in Cork who have been on this journey of discovery with me over many years; to Simon, Nollaig, Catherine, Kay, and Niamh much thanks. I wish to acknowledge my professional colleagues from the west of Ireland, Kathleen Fitzgerald, Jo Hanrahan, Madge Finn, and James Ronayne. To all the staff and students from the University of Limerick that I have worked with over the years, many thanks.

I wish to acknowledge and thank Penelope Easten, for her wisdom and her support over many years. Also the people who have shared their stories with me, and especially to those who have allowed me to publish their material so that we can all be better at what we do. Finally, to my wife, Jacinta, thank you for your love, ceaseless support, and encouragement, and to my two wonderful daughters, Siun and Aoileann, who I love more than anything in the world.

Finally, we would like to thank the editors of 'Context', the magazine for the Association for Family Therapy and the journal 'Attachment and Relational Psychoanalysis' for giving us permission to reprint images and content originally published in these journals.

Chapter 1

Transference and countertransference from an attachment perspective

Introducing the idea of a keystone system within the dynamic organization of the self

Transference is one of the most powerful processes through which we can know ourselves and be known by others. It has its roots in our earliest beginnings and our earliest responses to smell, taste touch, light, and sound. It happens out of conscious awareness and grows in complexity as we develop and experience the people and the environment we find ourselves living in. It is usually acted out or enacted in intimate or face-to-face relationships. It can also be triggered outside the domain of face-to-face contact. It can be sparked by the tone or pitch of a person's voice. It can be evoked by smell, colour, light, and the organization of physical space, buildings, landscape or seascape. It is a powerful phenomenon influencing one's internal emotional state and one's sense of equilibrium and belonging. At its most powerful it can influence our expectation of being known and liked by the other or the exact opposite.

This book expands our understanding of transference and countertransference. We approach the phenomenon of transference from an evolutionary perspective. By so doing we extend the domain of transferential phenomena from the purely internalized experiences of personal interactions to include (amongst others) such aspects of our biological makeup as our sexuality and the motivation and desire to construct a home that provides us with comfort, support, and pleasure. We base our thesis on the work of such theorists as Antonio Damasio, Peter Levine, Steven Porges, Daniel Stern, Colwyn Trevarthen, Ed Tronick and others who have studied communication at the cellular, biological, and interpersonal level.

We place our work solidly within the analytic tradition, particularly, to name a few, that of Ian Suttie, Ronald Fairbairn, Harry Guntrip, Enid and Michael Balint, and Donald Winnicott. We consider that the theoretical work of Dorothy Heard and Brian Lake, who built on the work of John Bowlby and located their understanding of human growth, development, and well-being within a biological framework, chimes with the work of these theorists. We consider that with the research carried out by Una McCluskey into affect attunement in adult psychotherapy and the practice she has developed for working with the dynamics of attachment in adult life, called exploratory goal-corrected psychotherapy, we have a useful map for practitioners which they can use to discern and tune into the meaning of what is being communicated to them in spite of the many hidden ways that this occurs.

The book is intended for psychologists, psychoanalytic psychotherapists of all persuasions, art therapists, nurses, social workers, counsellors, medical and legal personnel, organizational consultants, and teachers and people providing pastoral care or coaching. It is as relevant to the workplace manager, whether that is a professor in a university or a middle or senior manager working in an industrial setting, as to those in the health and social care professions.

We have two objectives, to introduce a theoretical frame for approaching the phenomenon of transference and countertransference and, secondly, to introduce a model of work that is being established within the attachment community, based on the work of Una McCluskey. The model is called exploratory goal-corrected psychotherapy (EGCP), or exploratory goal-corrected consultations (EGCC). It can be used as a guide for individual, couple, family, group, and organizational work.

John Bowlby was the first to notice that biologically based interpersonal systems were goal-corrected. He noticed that if a child was distressed and sought proximity to his or her primary caregiver, then, after a sufficient length of time with that caregiver, the behaviour of careseeking ceased and the child returned to what they were doing before they became distressed. He called the cessation of the arousal of a motivational system, in this case careseeking, goal-correction. In other words, careseeking behaviour had reached its goal and had now shut down until the next alarm or alert, which would trigger the motivation to find a caregiver all over again.

Part of Bowlby's initial unpopularity with his colleagues was that he seemed to dismiss the role of emotion in these interpersonal transactions and instead used semi-technical language, such as systems, goals, and goal-correction. Of course, Bowlby was well aware of the presence of emotion as a motivational force in the systems he had identified. To quote from his Maudsley lecture given in 1976 to the Royal College of Psychiatrists: 'Many of the most intense emotions arise during the formation, the maintenance, the disruption and the renewal of attachment relationships' (Bowlby, 1979, p.130).

Nevertheless, the concept of goal-correction in terms of how biologically based interpersonal systems work, which was central to Bowlby's theory of attachment, has tended to be overshadowed by the huge amount of interest and research based on Mary Ainsworth's (Ainsworth et al., 1969, 1974, 1978) use of the idea of a 'secure base' and subsequent stratification of attachment status at one year of age. We consider Ainsworth's work to be extremely important and to have made a substantial contribution to our understanding of the interior life of children and what they require in terms of personal relationships and stability for promoting their growth and development.

We agree with Heard and Lake (1997) that the ensuing emphasis by researchers and clinicians on classifying a child or adult's 'attachment style' as secure or insecure has taken the focus off what it means for a person's physical and mental health when the goals of biological individual and interpersonal aspects of the self are not met, or, in other words, fail to reach their biological goals. From their original publication on the dynamics of adult attachment, Heard and Lake (1986) over time enlarged the focus of Bowlby's and Ainsworth's work and drew our attention to a further five aspects of the self that were involved in this dynamic, four of which were also goal-corrected. The individual and interpersonal goal-corrected aspects of the self that they identified were: (i) a defensive self; (ii) an interest sharing self with peers; (iii) a sexual self; (iv) a self that is motivated to create a supportive external environment; and (v) a system within the self which has been described variously by analysts and others as the internal world. Heard and Lake (1997) originally called this our internalized experience of relationship (IMER) but settled in their 2009 book for the term 'internal environment', which they considered could be supportive or unsupportive of the self. This system is not goal-corrected. We go into a lot more detail about the internal environment of the self in Chapter Seven.

Heard and Lake called the theory underpinning their work the theory of attachment-based exploratory interest sharing (TABEIS). They described it as such in order to draw attention to the fact that, without the assuagement of careseeking, a person's capacity for exploratory interest sharing with peers was compromised. Dorothy Heard was the first to notice that there was a connection between the way a caregiver interacted with a distressed careseeker and the extent to which the careseeker was able to return to their former level of exploratory play. Successful interaction between the caregiver and the careseeker resulted in creative exploratory play. Unsuccessful interaction meant the careseeker remained distressed and play got put on hold or was resumed in a desultory or defensive fashion. In their last publication, written with McCluskey, Heard and Lake (2009/ 2012) considered that these seven aspects of the self worked together as a single process whose function was to create as much well-being as possible for the person. They called this the Restorative Process.

Heard and Lake's perspective on attachment and the way they have developed Bowlby's work is very different from other attachment theorists and allows us to see that the way in which a person may use biologically based aspects of themselves – which have their own discrete and separate goals (for example, sexuality) to regulate pain, distress and fear/dread – when seeking effective care from another person is not an option for one reason or another. Using an aspect of the self, which is designed for a particular purpose or purposes, primarily for the purpose of defending against pain and distress can have a profound effect on a person's life. This book addresses precisely this phenomenon. We explore the self from the point of view of the effect on the person's life when basic interpersonal systems embedded within the nature of the self fail to reach their biological goals.

In the 2009/12 book written by Heard, Lake and McCluskey, Chapter Two is devoted to describing our understanding of the self as containing the paradox of being experienced by the person as both autonomous and embedded in relationships. So, the aspects of the self that are embedded in relationships are: our careseeking selves; our caregiving selves; our defensive selves; our sexual selves; our interest sharing selves; and the part of us that can put together a physical home base that can support us when alone and enhance our well-being when with others.

By lack of resolution we mean that aspects of the self will have become aroused but not reached their goal. For example, a person may have the desire to create and build a supportive home base but submit to the taste and aesthetic of another person. In this way they renege on their own desires and put up with a home environment that is not of their choosing. They may not even be aware that this is what they have done and they may be completely out of touch with the effect this has had and is having on their state of well-being. On the other hand, they may well be aware of what has happened and be in touch with their discomfort, distress, and dissatisfaction but be unaware that what they are dealing with is the working of a basic system, which we all have, that desires to reach its own particular goal and that is not going to go away through the passing of time.

While taste in terms of house and home is derived from within the particular life experiences of the individual, many of our other systems are interpersonal and require an appropriately attuned and empathic response from another person in order to properly reach their biological goal. Different systems within the self will activate specific behaviours. When the goal is not reached, the connection between the behaviours and the system that is activated gets lost. Forever forward, the behaviours and the goal get disconnected. We act, of course we do, but we no longer have the experience of relief or joy or pleasure of having reached the goal of the part of the self that remains aroused within us. We know from talking to people in their eighties or nineties that they can still be mourning a lost relationship with someone from their youth, their homeland, or where they considered their true home to be; talents which they did not develop; children that they did not conceive or bring to term; children they feel they failed in terms of their caregiving; care they have desired and feel they have sought, but which was never received. Such disconnections are at the heart of what this book sets out to explore.

However, it is not just that individual aspects of the self fail to reach their potential. This is bad enough and a real tragedy in the life of a person, but it also means that these aspects of the self (i.e., caregiving or interest sharing), on being recruited to regulate distress caused by failure in another aspect of the self, are now hidden from the self and remain in need of care and attention in their own right. This is where the power of transferential communication comes in, but it requires that the therapist or caregiver be attuned to the nature of what it is they are picking up. So, for example, a person may present burnt out or overwhelmed by the amount of care they are providing to family, friends, and maybe also in their work. What may be going on here is a reliance on the caregiving aspect of themselves as a way of compensating for the lack of recognition, affect attunement, and affect regulation of their exploratory interest sharing self. Focusing on helping them to reduce the amount of care they give to others will not significantly alter the dynamic established at the core of the person and may miss completely what they actually need to pursue their interest sharing lives. We are suggesting that powerful motivational forces, fuelled by past unresolved aspects of the self, can play havoc with our lives and radically influence our capacity for living creatively and responding generously to the living nature of the world of which we are a part.

Transference and countertransference from an attachment perspective

At the centre of this book is the idea that when intrapersonal or interpersonal systems (aspects of the self) get aroused, the behaviour that follows is only logically and meaningfully connected when the system (aspect of the self) reaches its goal. When these logical and meaningful connections between the system and behaviour are lost, then crucial information is occluded from the person and those around him or her. We wish to suggest that a therapist, social worker, medical person, psychologist or anyone approached by a person in acute distress seeking help may find it useful to think, firstly, of the way in which this person is approaching them, secondly, they should consider the way we as professional caregivers respond to how the other presents, and, thirdly, consider the pattern of interaction between the careseeker and the caregiver, in the sense that both engage immediately in a pattern of interaction designed to conceal or reveal the nature of the person's distress. This map is a guide for the therapist in helping the person who seeks their help understand their behaviour in the here and now and how it has its origins in their earliest interactions with primary caregivers in earlier life.

The first point is about the way the other presents; i.e., is it angrily, or are they minimizing the problem, what is their tone of voice? We would consider these behavioural approaches to be manifestations of the defensive self, in flight or fight mode, what Stephen Porges would call the arousal of the mobilization circuit of the vagus nerve. This is not to suggest that the person presenting in this way to a doctor or social worker is aware that they are doing so defensively; it is simply the way they relate to a would-be caregiver. So, paying attention to the verbal and non-verbal presentation of the other is important.

Then there is the way we as professional caregivers respond to how the other presents. Someone having a coronary incident, for instance, may present with physiological arousal levels that show no indication that this event is taking place and so no visible signs show up on some measures. In other words, they have resorted unconsciously; i.e., their body has responded outside voluntary control to a strategy well used over many years, probably of shutting down their physiological arousal levels when they have experienced a life threat. They are using what

Porges refers to as the ancient reptilian immobilization system, another circuit of the vagus nerve, and are recruiting this system in defence of the self. This defensive strategy, coupled with a minimizing attitude and behaviour designed to miscue the caregiver, in this case the doctor, can mean that a true diagnosis is missed. A doctor or medical person who fails to detect the underlying stress and this parti-cular careseeking approach, which doesn't look like careseeking at all and can sometimes be experienced by the doctor as caregiving to them, will respond in such a way that the pattern of relating established between them and the patient is very unlikely to reach the goals of care that is at the heart of the transaction. So, the pattern established between the careseeker and caregiver is important.

Finally, there is the nature of what is being communicated by the other and the pattern of interaction established between them. We are suggesting that a therapist who is tuned in to the full range of biological interpersonal systems that are designed to enable a person to survive with well-being and vitality has a very useful and simple map to guide their work. This map relates to the many aspects of the self that may be presenting to the caregiver as unre-solved. Furthermore, the language we use to describe such aspects of the self – careseeking, caregiving, sexuality, defence, and so on – is easy to understand and makes complete sense to people.

The concept of transference that we are using in this book is extended from its original meaning. People communicate primarily through narrative. Narrative allows the attuned therapist using the model presented in this book to key into the particular aspect of the self that is being recruited in the service of defence at the expense, in some cases, of other aspects of the person and their well-being as a whole. People communicate through the projection of feeling and affective states, projection of their bodily tension and distress. This book provides not only a map to the territory one might explore with the client and why one might do that, but it is also a guide for exploration of the many hidden ways people communicate what concerns them most. This happens in the realm of what we call the transference. Sometimes we pick up information from the other by what they say or don't say, sometimes by how they say it, sometimes by how we feel, sometimes by how we want to act, sometimes by experiences we have in our body

The map we present focuses on key aspects of a person's life:

1   Who do they go to for care and support?
2   Who do they provide care for?
3   Who are they intimate with?
4   What interests do they have and do they share any of these with people who ignite their intelligence, competence, capacity, and aesthetic?
5   Do they have a home that supports their well-being?

What makes change slow and problematic is that, when people are distressed and need help, their previous experience of those in a caregiving role will be brought to bear as the lens through which to engage with and predict how their current caregiver is going to respond to them. It is imperative that professional caregivers are aware of this and have some competence in how to negotiate this tricky terrain.

The purpose of this book is:

1   To provide therapists and clients with a map for exploration once they engage in work together.
2   To provide a guide to explore which aspect of the self is linked with the distress being presented.
3   To examine how to maintain an open exploratory process so that meaning evolves in the space between careseeker and caregiver, rather than being predicted or constrained by theoretical dogma.

A keystone system at the centre of well-being: a focus for the transference

Having spent nearly twenty-five years exploring and researching Heard and Lake's work in relation to extending and developing attachment theory as presented by John Bowlby and his followers, McCluskey considers that when these systems are not resolved (in the sense of having reached their goal) then one of the seven systems that make up the Restorative Process (outlined by Heard, Lake & McCluskey 2009/2012) can act as a keystone in the overall balance in the life that the person achieves for him or herself. The idea of a keystone system incorporates the concept that a person can feel or believe that their survival with well-being is determined by whether this system is functioning as well as is possible for them and that an attack, assault or loss of the possibility of meeting to some extent the goal of that system can feel calamitous. The system occupying this position is likely to be the chief system recruited in the service of defence. It is likely to be the behaviour that has achieved some level of validation, praise, and recognition, and through which the person experiences some level of competence and control. However, the keystone system acts as a decoy for the person and takes them away from the true nature of their distress.

In McCluskey's work with professional caregivers, who have attended her courses on 'exploring the dynamics of attachment in adult life' (see Chapter Nine), she has seen this phenomenon at work over and over again. What she has noticed is that one of the innate behavioural biological systems identified by Heard and Lake takes priority over the others in a way that the person feels gives meaning to their life, but where they can simultaneously feel depleted, burnt out, and unfulfilled as a person. She is calling this phenomenon an overreliance on a keystone system.

It is this idea of a keystone system that works to occlude from consciousness the state of a person's true distress that gives us leverage to extend the concept of transference and countertransference that traditionally has belonged within the analytic tradition and locates it within an attachment or biologically based inter-personal perspective. The idea of a keystone system allows us to think that a person may function primarily from the basis of using one of the biologically based aspects of the relational self to sustain well-being. The person will prioritize that aspect of their life at the expense of all others. For example, someone with an unresolved careseeking self might prioritize caregiving to others. In this case, their caregiving self becomes their keystone system.

A keystone system for another person might be their 'personally created external environment'; we explore how this can work out in Chapter Three. Another might prioritize interest sharing with peers. Approaching interests as a way of distracting oneself from a failure to reach the goal of a different aspect of the self, which requires effective engagement with another person, is likely to result in a dominant or submissive mode of relating to others. A person may have found that the only way to get another to pay attention to them is to try to coax or bully them into engagement. This may show up in a person not being able to look for a peer, someone they would consider their equal in terms of stamina, intelligence, and capacity to deal with fear. They may approach others from a sense of feeling that the other will always want to control them in a way that they must resist. Only when that person meets someone with whom he or she feels safe and who they experience as not trying to dominate, bully or steal from them will their creativity flourish in the context of this new interest sharing relationship.

When one system acts as a key system for the person, other aspects of the self are affected as well. For example, our sexual selves, or indeed our moti-vation to create a supportive home base, may be recruited to manage and regulate physiological arousal that is unregulated at source. Having to use interpersonal aspects of the self in this way in order to maintain as much well-being as possible may mean that our capacity to live a creative life may be put on the back burner or avoided altogether. It is important to remember that, from the perspective of the attachment model being presented here, we con-sider that a person only resorts to this defensive use of self when they have not had the supports they need to grow and thrive without undue fear in the world in which they find themselves.

We consider that a person can be helped to reduce their reliance on their key-stone system but that this is long-term and delicate work with an attuned and exploratory other. We provide a case example in Chapter Five. Change in the dynamic organization of the self (in other words, how the seven systems in the Restorative Process interact together) happens, in our view, through a particular kind of interaction with another person (in this context, a therapist/caregiver). We explore in great detail how this works in the following chapters. The nature of this relationship is at the core of the model we present in this book and which we consider contributes to clinical practice. We call this practice exploratory goal-corrected psychotherapy (EGCP). As mentioned earlier, the caregiver's focus is on the verbal, physical, and affective communication from the careseeker. The title of this model of practice, EGCP, accurately reflects the process of interaction between the therapist and client, or careseeker and caregiver. Both are working together to meet the goals of basic interpersonal systems.

Security as a function of goal-correction of the careseeking system

We take seriously the idea that children develop strategies of relational behaviour when seeking care in response to different types of caregiving responses they have experienced. Some of these strategies are defensive, designed to protect the self from having experienced undesired or painful responses. In general, these strategies take place at an involuntary level – they are instinctive. The non-defensive form enables the developing child to accurately read other people's emotive signals, to approach them for help when required, and to allow the other to regulate their emotion and provide them with necessary skills to solve intra-personal or interpersonal issues in such a way that they have the experience of returning fully to what they were doing before they became frightened or alarmed. We call this child secure. From the perspective being offered in this book, we consider that security is a function of goal-correction of the careseeking system. When the motivational system to reach for care from another person is followed through and successfully met by a responsive caregiver, the careseeker has the experience of their goal being met and the motivational system that became aroused returns to neutral until another event triggers anxiety or alarm – the system is goal-corrected.

The defensive form makes it difficult for the child to communicate clearly their distress or to read accurately the affect being expressed on the other person's face or tone of voice. This has been widely researched by such people as Gergely (1992), Gergely and Fonagy (1998), Hofer (1983), Schore (1994) and Porges (2007).

The insecure patterns can take the form of avoiding contact with others when frightened or needing emotional/practical help. It can also take the form of ambivalent behaviours, apparently seeking help and care but resisting it at the same time. Another form of defensive relational behaviour is to become frozen, unable to think clearly or take action. Another form of relational behaviour when frightened or in need of help is to become disorganized. Unlike the other forms just described, this behaviour has no organizational structure, it has no identifiable pattern to it, and it is, as it says, disorganized (see Solomon & George, 1999; Solomon & George, 1991; Crittenden, 2006). In extreme circumstances people and animals will shut down all vital functions so that they are maintaining survival at a minimal level. It generally signifies that the person has experienced extreme trauma. We see this as the central nervous system responding automatically to what the person perceives as a life threat, and agree with Stephen Porges who suggests that when earlier evolutionary-based defence systems are recruited in the service of managing interpersonal trauma they have a profound effect on the physiological, as well as the psychological, well-being of the person. For the professional caregiver this means that he or she has to be aware of the transferential information they are receiving from the careseeker through their own body responses, and work with this information appropriately. We develop these ideas in Chapter Nine.

One sees the corollary of these presentations in adults when they present for therapy (McCluskey, 2005, Chapter Eleven), and it is from this research and our subsequent practice experience – Michael's from his private practice with individuals seeking therapy, Una's from her work with psychotherapists, psychologists, and others in the caring professions who have explored their own attachment dynamics in confidential closed groups – that we examine transference and countertransference from an attachment perspective and offer our findings as a guide for clinical practice.

These defensive patterns of relational organization are clear examples of a system being aroused (e.g., careseeking), but the behaviour derived from the arousal of the system is illogical.

So, we have basically three patterns of relating when our defensive self is aroused. These correspond to what Porges has identified as the phylogenetically organized evolution of the vagus nerve, which he elaborated through what he called his polyvagal theory. This refers to the vagus nerve, which has three circuits organized in a hierarchy. The newer circuit controls the social engagement system. In our model, careseeking is expressed through this nervous system. It relates to the myelinated part of the vagus nerve which controls facial muscles, voice tone, listening. If this circuit fails to regulate the person and restore the person to a sense of safety, the body can recruit the second level of defence, which is the second circuit of the vagus nerve. The second circuit controls information to and from the brain to the organs above the diaphragm and is involved in the behaviours of fight, flight, and freeze. Porges refers to this as the mobilization system. If these behaviours fail to restore a sense of safety to the person, the body recruits a third level of defence. This is the third circuit of the vagus nerve and is the older system used by our reptilian ancestors to defend against life-threatening situations and involves shutting down and becoming immobilized. In our experience, traumatic experiences can often elicit this third level of defence and affect people's physical health.

Porges' social engagement system describes how we communicate to one another through facial expression, voice tone, prosody, listening, and so on. It is involved in the to-and-fro communication from one person to another. When this is not working and the two people are missing each other or one person is frightening the other, then non-verbal communication is affected. Porges describes how it becomes more difficult to read each other's non-verbal signals. This is when the second circuit of the vagus nerve is involved. We then have fear infiltrating the attachment systems and we get a mode of relating to the other which is expressed by trying to dominate the other or by giving in to them: dominant vs. submissive (Heard & Lake, 1997). This mode of relating will be present in whichever system is aroused – interest sharing, sexuality, caregiving, or careseeking.

The development of a research relationship between Heard, Lake and McCluskey

Heard and Lake's unique contribution to a theory of human development is this observation that the seven systems interact with one another to enable the person to achieve as much well-being as possible. Well-being will be a function of knowing that there is someone or several people you can count on to respond when you need help and support; knowing that the relationship is tried and tested and will deliver unless the other is in a position where they are unable to respond for some reason. Well-being is a function of having a peer or many different peers one can share one's interests with and with whom one can develop new skills. Contact with one's peers brings new levels of vitality and enhances one's sense of being alive and being part of this world. Well-being is knowing that one can provide protective or exploratory care for those with whom one has a strong affectionate bond. Well-being is having a close intimate relationship where each can appreciate and enjoy the other's physicality and sexuality. Well-being is creating a home from which one derives great pleasure. Well-being is having a supportive internal sense of self in the world. And, finally, well-being is a function of knowing that one has a robust capacity to take care of oneself, that one's two systems for self-defence (mobilization and immobilization) work beautifully on their own when required to do so and that one's capacity to careseek from responsive and capable people is in good working order.

Dorothy Heard worked in the department of children and parents at the Tavistock Clinic in London with John Bowlby as a consultant child psychiatrist for over twenty years between the 1950s and 1970s so was very familiar with his work, and that of Ainsworth and others who were part of the research and clinical team in Bowlby's department. From the late 1970s, Heard and Lake lived in Yorkshire and were members of a research team based at the University of York for the study of attachment and object relations. Heard had already published papers linking object relations theory with attachment dynamics, (Heard, 1978, 1982). McCluskey was a member of that team so knew their work well. By the time she had completed her own research and explored in depth the dynamics involved in goal-corrected empathic attunement (GCEA) and started to investigate their work in 2006, they had extended their understanding of attachment to its current position (Heard, Lake & McCluskey, 2009/12). At this point they had seen that LeDoux's work on the fear system needed to be integrated with Bowlby's work on the careseeking system, as both these systems were key for survival. In their earlier book, published in 1997, they had drawn extensively on

MacLean's (1990) theory of the triune brain. This they abandoned in their 2009/2012 publication due to advances in brain imagery, which revealed that various regions of the brain are active during primal, emotional, and relational experiences, showing that Maclean's view of the brain represented an over-simplification of brain structure and functioning.

We integrate the work of Porges and Damasio into Heard and Lake's understanding of the personal system for self-defence. We find helpful Porges' understanding of the three circuits of the vagus nerve, particularly the old vagus circuit that delivers information to and from the organs below the diaphragm and is aroused in situations experienced as a threat to life. We find this makes sense in our experience of working with highly traumatized individuals, where the work is primarily with the body, the information held in the body, and how that information is transferred to the bodies of others, particularly in the context of working with a group (see Chapter Seven). Damasio's (2018) privileging of the role of emotion as our basic source of information, coupled with the work of Porges (1994), provides a scientific basis for what we experience in the consulting room and the practice that we have developed to regulate the other when they revisit experiences too traumatic and disorganizing to integrate.

Dorothy Heard said to McCluskey on many occasions that the evidence of progress in therapy is when the careseeker begins to actively seek help from the therapist. It took her a while to understand that Heard meant the careseeker had to change their style of seeking help and be able to approach without fear and without defensive strategies such as appeasing or looking after their caregiver as 'payment' for seeking care. Heard clearly understood that the pivotal system within the overall Restorative Process was the careseeking system, and that if that was dysfunctional it had a significant effect on the organization of the whole.

McCluskey found evidence for this some years later when she carried out research on the courses she was running for professional caregivers. The key factor in promoting well-being turns out to be a change in careseeking behaviour (see McCluskey & Gunn, 2015). Clearly then, change in the careseeking system is the driver for change in the overall organization of the person. This is such an important finding that it is our wish it be researched more fully and that would-be professional caregivers become aware of just how important effective careseeking is to overall health and well-being.

So, to get back to the idea of a keystone system, while it would appear that the way the careseeking system functions is key to overall levels of well-being, McCluskey's observations led her to think, as mentioned earlier, that people prioritize different systems, albeit unconsciously, in the service of their own state of well-being. It is important to remember that if careseeking is unassuaged then all the other systems are going to be infiltrated to some degree by the fear form of the system for self-defence (mobilization and immobilization). For instance, if person A prioritizes caregiving it is likely that the caregiving they provide has certain limitations and may not withstand too much challenge to the form in which it is offered. Alan Bennett's play 'Hallelujah' (2018) is a good example of defensive caregiving within the health service. We explore this dynamic in great detail in Chapter Nine.

In addition, the caregiver is likely to be overwhelmed by their inability to refuse careseeking requests and may well be unaware that they are heading towards burnout, as caregiving for them is their keystone system. Their identity depends on it. For someone else it will be interest sharing, for another sexuality, and so on. We think that the idea of a keystone system sits within the Restorative Process and can help us as therapists discern from the myriad verbal and non-verbal communications coming to us from our clients which is the key system they are presenting to us for exploration, however hidden this communication is. This is where our understanding of transference and countertransference within an attachment perspective comes to the fore.

Connecting with a person's affective experience

When the careseeking system is aroused, the person requires a responsive cooperative caregiver; otherwise the person has no hope of reaching the goal of their careseeking system (certainly not until they are old enough to have internalized a responsive, effective caregiver and are physically capable of obtaining what they want). If the person fails to get the response they require from the other person (their perceived caregiver) the careseeking system is not resolved and so remains active, fuelling behaviour that will now be infiltrated by the careseeker's system for self-defence. An exploratory, undefended caregiver will attune to the person's affective experience and regulate their distress in spite of their defensive presentations, which could include being angry with or withdrawn from the caregiver. It is this responsive interaction with the person in distress that regulates the careseeking system and assuages the more automatic and unconscious forms of self-defence.

In the absence of a regulatory response from a caregiver to the affect being presented, the person has got to find a way to manage the emotional distress of not having their needs met and they will resort to relying on their own resources. The person's subsequent behaviour towards potential caregivers (because their behaviour is no longer clear and straightforward, being infiltrated by defence mechanisms) is unlikely to achieve the original goal, thereby continuing to leave the person in distress; the origins of which may be known or unknown to them. They are more likely to build up a plethora of evidence, based on these failed experiences of getting the responses they require, to form a belief that they are better off managing life's problems on their own, without the help of others. Edith Eger, a survivor of the Nazi concentration camps who went on to become a psychotherapist in later life, has written extensively about this phenomenon in her book, 'The Choice' (Eger, 2017). While she uses a different paradigm for understanding why people get stuck in old patterns of relating, her case studies exemplify the thinking being put forward here. Eger gives examples of how she enabled people to resolve past trauma from her own extensive life experience.

It is this idea – that biological systems, and the behaviours that are derived from them, may lose their meaningful connection – that is at the heart of this book. If behaviour can get detached from the arousal of particular aspects of the self, so that the behaviour as expressed is no longer logically related to enabling that aspect of the self to reach its goal, it may be helpful, if the person is willing and curious, to explore the lost connection and the roots in the arousal of one or another of the biological systems. This has the possibility of providing the person with a sense that they can make the necessary changes in their lives and to seek out the help they require to do so. The key dynamic underpinning this change seems to be the enabling of the person to see a separation between their biological behavioural systems and the self.

The McCluskey model for exploring the dynamics of attachment in adult life, a guide for practice

For the past twenty plus years McCluskey has been developing a model for working with the dynamics of attachment in adults, using a theory of interaction for caregiving (McCluskey, 2001) and a theory of attachment-based exploratory interest sharing (Heard, Lake & McCluskey, 2009/12). This has become known as the McCluskey model for exploring the dynamics of attachment in adult life.

Her initial research, inspired by the work of Murray and Trevarthen (1985, 1986) and Daniel Stern (1985) on affect attunement in adult psychotherapy (McCluskey, Roger & Nash, 1997; , Hooper & Bingley Miller, 1999) had alerted her to the idea that the 'offer to treat' (i.e., to caregive) aroused the dynamics of attachment in both the seeker and provider, whether they be a therapist or a taxi driver, if the person seeking help is in distress. With this in mind, she set out to test that idea and found some evidence to support it, including that training could make a difference to the dynamic of interaction.

In addition, she found that the interaction between a careseeker and a caregiver when successful (in terms of the careseeker feeling relief, met and understood) was goal-corrected, meaning that the behaviour ceased once the person experienced the goal of that behavioural system being met. She went on to create measures of the experience of the interaction between the two parties. She found that on completion of the interview these measures (completed separately by the careseeker and the caregiver) correlated with each other to a statistically significant degree if the experience was felt as a success, and similarly if the experience was felt as a failure.

Analysis of the audio-visual data of the interaction (examined in detail at the rate of 25 frames a second) showed that there were typically five different presentations of careseeking and five different presentations of caregiving, yielding twenty-five patterns of interaction between the dyads. Only two of these were successful in terms of enabling the careseeker to explore their situation. Further analysis revealed that the process of interaction in the effective patterns of interaction involved what she termed goal-corrected empathic attunement (GCEA).

This is all described in detail in the book 'To be Met as a Person' (McCluskey, 2005). GCEA is the process through which the two goal-corrected systems of caregiving and careseeking reach their respective goals (McCluskey, Hooper & Bingley Miller, 1999).

By then she had a description of the careseeking and caregiving presentations and it seemed clear to her (after lengthy analysis of video material stretching over two years) that she had the adult equivalent of the secure and insecure patterns of attachment described by Ainsworth and her followers. She now sees that she had more than that. She had a detailed account of facial characteristics when the immobilization system was active in both parties. When she discussed her work with Allan Shore at his home in 2004, she can now see, he saw more in her research than she did herself at that time. She was not aware that Porges had identified the myelinated part of the vagus nerve which was implicated in face-to-face emotional expression and attunement to the state the other is in.

She now had (i) a theoretical understanding of the dynamics of interaction in therapeutic situations between what she then termed careseekers and caregivers (the attachment system as described by Bowlby), (ii) a formulation of the nature of the interaction between the caregiver and the careseeker which would assuage careseeking and allow for the careseeker to engage in exploration (GCEA), and (iii) a model of training for practitioners interested in this way of working. This has resulted in developing a model of therapeutic work called exploratory goal-corrected psychotherapy (EGCP) and a training programme designed to equip people to understand and respond to micro-communication at the verbal and non-verbal level.

We now consider that GCEA is the process through which the caregiver enables the careseeker to reach the goal of not only the systems of careseeking and caregiving, but of each of the other systems (aspects of the self) involved in the Restorative Process identified by Heard and Lake. For the reader's benefit, and for clarity, we repeat these other aspects of the self are the sexual self, the interest sharing self, the defensive self, the supportive or unsupportive internal environment, and the supportive or unsupportive personally created external environment.

These systems are as different as interest sharing with peers is from sexuality, as the personally created external environment is from the system for caregiving or self-defence. They are all unique and different, and have different effects on a person's sense of well-being, contentment, and creativity when they reach or fail to reach their goal.

A note on how we have approached the writing of this book

We have both worked on all the chapters. When drawing on our own practice, we indicate this in the text.

Chapter 2

The dynamics of attachment in adult life

A version of this chapter originally appeared in 'Context' (McCluskey, 2010), the magazine for the Association for Family Therapy. The purpose was to give a brief introduction to the work of Heard and Lake and the practice developed therefrom by Una McCluskey; Exploring the Dynamics of Attachment in Adult Life, a course for professional caregivers. It is reproduced in part here in order to give the reader an overview of the theoretical background we are using to explore the concept of transference and countertransference. We outline in simple terms the nature of the seven systems constituting the Restorative Process and how they work together to maintain a particular level of well-being for the person.

We start with the story of someone who was a Catholic priest. He said once that he kept himself sane through his many interests. He shared these activities with others who were equally interested in these pursuits. He had serious interests in music, gardening, and photography and organized his home accordingly. Much later in his life, while recovering from a major illness, he turned once again to interests as he made his recovery and developed a high level of competence in wood turning, inlay, and furniture making.

These interests affected his mood and his vitality, and gave him pleasure and self-esteem in his own eyes and in the world of his peers. When he understood that I was taking a professional interest in the dynamics of human behaviour, he discussed with me the fact that maintaining his interests affected his vitality and well-being and helped him cope with the loneliness inherent in his lack of an affectionate sexual relationship, which was part of the commitment required of a celibate priest.

In these ways my friend exemplified that the manner in which a person handles a basic biological drive – in this case for sex – can be related to activities and perceptions which we regard as cultural and more distinctively human. My friend's account resonated with the many years I have spent working as an individual, couple, family, and group therapist (Haldane & McCluskey, 1977, 1980a, 1980b, 1982, 1993; Haldane, McCluskey & Peacey, 1980; McCluskey, 1983, 1987, 1990, 2002, 2003, 2005, 2007a, 2007b, 2008, 2010, 2011a, 2011b; McCluskey & Bingley Miller, 1995). During this time I had struggled to find a way of understanding what I was experiencing in practice, which was the manner in which the different facets of people's lives (which I now understand as biological systems) intertwined and affected the person's experience and competence.

I also had a keen interest in developing methods of working with people that were effective at engaging the emotional effects of the events that happened to them, and the effect of unprocessed emotional experiences on their mental and physical health, their relationships, work, and sense of competence (McCluskey, 1987, 2001, 2003, 2005, 2007a, 2008; McCluskey & Bingley Miller, 1995). While working with Dr Douglas Haldane, consultant child psychiatrist (Haldane & McCluskey, 1977, 1980a, 1980b, 1982, 1993; Haldane, McCluskey & Peacey, 1980), we were repeatedly aware when working with couples that attention to one aspect of their lives, such as how they handled the organization of their home and finances, could resolve other aspects of their lives, such as their sexual relationship. What we did not have then, to make sense of our experience, was a theoretical frame that understood persons from a biological perspective and could offer some account for the distress caused when biological systems fail to reach their goal and which would also provide an explanation for how helping a person reach the goal of one of their biological systems could enable change in the organization of the self as a whole.

How the seven systems relate to one another

As my example of the Catholic priest was intended to show, these different systems, while independent of each other, are also connected. The careseeking system becomes active, along with the system for self-defence, when the person senses or experiences a threat to well-being. The third system, the internal environment, is triggered simultaneously. Once the person's careseeking system has been activated along with their fear system (which is part of their defensive self), their capacity for caregiving will be compromised, as will their capacity for developing and sharing interests and engaging in a mutually satisfying sexual relationship. If on their own, and having no access to a person they experience as supportive, they will rely on their internal and their personally created external environment, which they will experience as either supportive or unsupportive.

Our internal environment is particularly important in therapy and is dealt with in more detail in Chapter Six. Our external environment is the home we have created for ourselves to live in; it may be as small as one room, but it is created and fashioned in a way that is designed to provide support for the self as a whole, or for a particular specially valued aspect of the self. The external environment we create may serve to defend the self against the awareness of painful experiences, or may promote our well-being and creative potential. This is elaborated on fully in the coming chapter.

As already described, the seven systems are biological and six of them are goal-corrected. They are influenced in terms of motivation to reach their goal by the memory of how the person has been related to in the past (which is stored in the internal environment). Thus a person's careseeking system may be aroused at a point of crisis, but may be overridden by the fear system (influenced by the internal environment which is keeping a record of how the self was responded to in the past). This may mean that the person does not seek help when needed, or may do so inappropriately. Instead, the fear system will be expressed by the behaviours: flight (submission-avoidance), fight and flight (dominance/submission-ambivalence), fight (dominance), freeze (disorganization), or Porges' third circuit of the vagus nerve, immobilization, feigning death.

If the person has a history of approaching for help when they were frightened or distressed, and have then had the experience of being dismissed, ridiculed, neglected, abused or ignored, they will be left with the job of regulating their state of fear on their own. They may do this by withdrawing into rocking, head-banging, self-clasping, self-stimulating, collapsing, singing, lulling themselves into a trance-like state, praying, meditating, dissociating – all manner of self-soothing and self-regulating activities (Tronick, 1989; Tronick & Cohn, 1989).

In addition to the withdrawal described above (the flight aspect of the self-defence system), the person might try to influence their caregiver to attend to them, either through the defensive form of caregiving – where they seek to take care of the caregiver in order to get some positive attention – or they might try to dominate their caregiver into giving them what they want (using the fight aspect of their fear system). All these behaviours are defensive; they defend the self from the unbearable feeling of being left alone and not mattering to anyone else. In more serious cases of neglect and abuse, the person may recruit the third circuit of the vagus nerve as described by Steven Porges to maintain their survival with as much well-being as possible, even though this may be having a serious impact on their physical health.

In an unregulated state – where the person has not been helped by another human being to cope with unbearable emotion – a person can discover that they can relieve their fear by dominating the other and making them suffer the pain of rejection or abuse (physical, sexual or emotional) either through acting these behaviours out in reality, or in fantasy. Such behaviour has the effect of restoring some sense of control and vitality. If a person adopts this mode of interacting when threatened, then they will discover that by being dominant (the bully), either in reality or in fantasy, they do not have to live with the constant experience of fear. In some cases they may be able to avoid the experience of fear altogether.

In all these behaviours the proper functioning of the attachment system is distorted – the person has given up on careseeking. The person is at the mercy of their fear system, which is infiltrating all other aspects of their life – their capacity for caregiving, their interest sharing, and their capacity for affectionate sexuality.

A person who has not had their own careseeking needs met adequately may be capable of sympathy and empathy for other people, but to a limited degree. For example, once their caregiving is not well received, or is challenged, the person will tend to experience frustration or helplessness, and resort to either dominance (control – advice-giving in the main) or withdrawal as a way of dealing with their underlying state of fear and lack of competence (included or excluded from consciousness).

There is thus a crucial difference between what happens to the self when careseeking has been met and what happens to the self when it has not. When it has not been met, all the person's interpersonal systems are infiltrated by the defence system. When careseeking has been met, not only has the person's fear system been assuaged but the person has been given the skills to manage the situation, or the person who they have gone to for care has reminded them of their capacity to cope and their competence. They return to their interest sharing and their affectionate/sexual life; their exploratory, empathic caregiving capacity is restored to optimal functioning and they engage creatively with life through supportive companionable relations with others.

The internal environment

There is one system that is not goal-corrected; that is the system described as the 'internal environment'. How does that work, and how does it interact with the other systems? The internal environment (IE) of the self is triggered by 'lookalikes' (reminders) in the here and now to past experiences. The system (IE) is then activated and will be experienced by the self as supportive or unsupportive.

The following is an example of how the internal environment can be triggered and how a therapist can provide an opportunity for the self to expand consciousness of its own workings.

An adult is out walking and decides to pick up a few sticks, including a piece of an old hawthorn tree. This triggers a memory of being out on a walk with fellow scholars from boarding school, when suddenly there was a commotion up ahead – one of the 11-year-old children had apparently lost control and the teacher was giving her a horrific beating with a hawthorn stick. What is lodged in the internal environment is not only the incident, which may be recorded as a memory, but more important in terms of how this system works is the internalized experience (as a witness) of seeking or not seeking help to deal with this outrage to one's sensibilities, and the quality of the help received or not received.

It is this experience of interaction with one's caregiver that is lodged in the internal environment, providing support or lack of support for the self. This experience (amongst others) from the past (whether conscious of it or not) is triggered when one's fear system is aroused at a later date. This is an example of a response that has lost connection to its original source. What will have happened in the above example is that the child's system for self-defence – which includes the fear system and the careseeking system – will have become activated on witnessing the beating and hearing the sounds of pain. If the child does not receive effective caregiving (which must include attunement to the fear and regulation of the arousal state associated with fear) then they are at the mercy of an over-aroused physiological state that they will have to regulate as best they can (as described above). This they will do instinctively by using other aspects of themselves, such as a defensive form of sexuality, interests, religious practices or creating a defensive external environment designed to ward off bad and disturbing emotions.

The arousal of the fear system has to be assuaged by a caregiver before the person is available to respond with empathic, fear-free, supportive, companionable, educative caregiving. In the above example, from the point of view of the child who witnessed the beating, the adult available to soothe the fear system and provide effective caregiving is the same adult who is the source of the fear; a state of affairs likely to leave the child to self-regulate as best they can, especially in the absence of proximity to their regular caregiver (the child being at boarding school). The effectiveness of how the child deals with this scenario will be based on their internal environment and whether they have sufficient internalized positive regulating and educative experiences with their original or main caregiver to help them to manage the fear aroused by this incident.

The internal environment is constructed out of our experience of relationships with significant others (especially in childhood), how they have related to us, what they have called us, how they have treated us, the attributions they have ascribed to us. If we have experienced a lot of negative attributions ('Do you never listen or take anything in? Are you stupid or what?'; 'What a nuisance you are. Can't you see I am busy?'; 'You will bring disgrace upon the family – you will kill your mother/father – you are no good at anything – you are a cruel, thoughtless person'), these and other negative comments get lodged in the self and can come to form a core identity – how the self really perceives itself to be.

How is the internal environment connected with the other systems?

Think of the situation where one is at a meeting and discovers one has forgotten to bring certain documents or to check out important information that one had agreed to do, the consequences of which are likely to anger those present and to disrupt or delay the work. A person with a highly critical internal environment is immediately going to have their system for self-defence activated. They will attune to the anger and impatience of the others and, instead of mobilizing empathic caregiving and an exploratory capacity to repair and deal with the situation they are in, the person is likely instead to retreat into the fear aspect of self-defence. In this state, he or she loses touch with their capacity for careseeking (in its internalized form – the sense that there is and has always been a benign other available to help them). In this state (of not having an internalized effective caregiver who has mostly been able to remind them of their worth and competence), they are likely to lose competence and 'forget' the circumstances that led to them not carrying out their responsibilities. In addition, because they lose the capacity for empathy for those present at the meeting (and simply see them as critical attackers who find fault and want in the self) they are unable to engage in collaborative problem-solving. Instead they remain trapped in defence and in the survival of the self, trying to reclaim as much of a 'good name' for themselves as possible and fearful of the consequences; they are likely to be aggressive, become submissive or withdraw into a collapse.

Heard and Lake have made a truly original contribution to our understanding of the dynamics of self organization and development in the way they have brought many different aspects of people's lives together into one conceptualization. They have integrated a person's need and desire for care when distressed or frightened with a person's instinctive desire to care for someone they are attached to. They have linked the natural tendency to develop an interest and share it with one's peers with a natural instinct to love and express affection. They have linked the development of an effective system for self-defence with the way in which a caregiver provides education as well as support for a distressed careseeker. They have integrated LeDoux's (1998) fear system within the system for self-defence, but added into this system the careseeking system. They have built on Bowlby's idea of internal working models and have added in people's life-long interest in creating and sustaining a supportive environment in which to live.

Michael and I have built on this work to extend the system for personal self-defence by including the work of Porges and Damasio, which provides a coherent understanding of our practice with very traumatized individuals who, out of necessity, have had to rely on the older systems within the biological make-up of the person to survive as best they can. We have also introduced the idea of a keystone system which can help us to see and hear the significance of what seems to matter enormously to the other person but which can leave us a bit uncertain as to its significance and therefore unable to attune, empathize or respond appropriately.

In the next chapter we give an example of someone presenting with acute anxiety where the source of the anxiety was located in an aspect of the self that felt threatened: the personally created external environment.

Chapter 3

One's home base

The keystone system to be addressed as the source of the transference

This chapter focuses on the importance of paying attention to a person's home as the source of the transferential communication. One's 'found' environment, and subsequently the physical environment one creates for oneself, can have huge significance on a person's life and can sustain or undermine their well-being. What Heard and Lake referred to as the 'personally created external environment', a biologically based system that was individually goal-corrected based on early experience of important relationships, can, as McCluskey has conceptualized, act as a keystone system in maintaining well-being. We hope this chapter gives the reader a sense of what this means in the life of an individual and also conveys the way in which all seven systems interact together to give meaning to the behaviour and choices made by a person, given the challenges that life throws at them.

The story centres on a young woman called Rebekah, then in her mid-to-late thirties, who got lost in the middle of England while driving from her adopted home in the south of the country to Scotland, where she was to undertake postgraduate professional training, and the profound impact that losing her way had on her. At the time this happened she was an experienced and accomplished professional well used to travelling to unknown and varied places. But the panic experienced during this event was overwhelming and the memory haunts her and impacts her confidence to undertake journeys now in the later years of her life.

Rebekah's eleven years in Freudian analysis, where this event was recalled and worked with many times, failed to lessen the terror of such an event repeating itself or provide any understanding of why getting lost geographically in the middle of England at that point in her life had such an impact in the first place.

More than forty years after this had happened she approached me (McCluskey) for help as she was contemplating travelling north again, and the terror that she had experienced in the past was taking hold and paralyzing her. As she was recalling this incident I began to see that the issue here could be related to a biological system that was aroused and could be the source of the distress. I knew from her history that she had lost her original home when she was three and that at the time she made this journey she had, in effect, lost her home again.

I mentioned this and she immediately saw a connection that made sense to her and gave her relief. In the model being presented in this book, her careseeking system in relation to her unresolved feelings about this event had been met and she experienced relief. What was extraordinary, though, was the immediacy of the effect on her exploratory process.

Shortly after, she started to undertake many more journeys, still with some anxiety but she started travelling and doing more of what she wanted to do. It is true that there were other factors in Rebekah's life that made travel difficult over the years, but she agrees that the underlying terror related to leaving her home has substantially eased following the exchange referred to. Because it has had such a profound effect, she agreed to collaborate and work closely with me on unravelling what happened. She has an analytic background herself, though is unfamiliar with the attachment model presented here.

What happened between us was I noticed that the biological system that was aroused and was the source of her distress was the system for creating a supportive or unsupportive external environment, which in everyday language is the home one creates and relies on to sustain well-being. By recognizing this I was responding to the careseeking aspect of Rebekah that needed this aspect of herself (her need to create and have a supportive external environment) to be recognized.

Because this story illustrates the complex manifestations of transferential communication we go into great detail about this event in this chapter. It also brings to the fore the nature of the model we are presenting in this book on the understanding of transference from an attachment perspective.

The important thing to understand about transference from an attachment perspective is that what may be excluded from conscious awareness is the aspect of the self that is aroused and unregulated. A professional caregiver, working from an attachment perspective, will be on the lookout for the aspect of the self that is being presented for attention. It could be the internal environment, it could be the affectionate sexual self, or the interest sharing self, the defensive self or, as in this case, the personally created external environment.

Normally the term transference is reserved for interpersonal phenomena. In therapeutic circles it usually refers to feelings in relation to past relationships that are transferred to a therapist or analyst. While it can work both ways, it is normally considered as one-way traffic from client to therapist. It is assumed the therapist has had the chance while they were in training to spot such dynamics taking place between themselves and their clients and not act them out. It is understood within the trade that, with the insight gained from one's own analysis, one will be able to monitor one's reactions and respond in a helpful manner.

Countertransference usually refers to the therapist's ability to note and make sense of emotions he or she is experiencing in the presence of the client and to consider these as important, if unconscious, communication from the client.

We suggest that as well as transference within the interpersonal and intra-personal domain one can consider that a person can transfer feelings from other biological systems within the attachment dynamic, as described in Chapter Two.

I said in the Introduction that biological goal-corrected systems and the behaviour logically associated with meeting the goals of these systems can get disconnected. I am now suggesting that, as well as the meaning of the behaviour becoming occluded from a person's conscious awareness, the meaning of the feelings that the person experiences can suffer the same fate. The emotional experience in the moment may well be connected with an earlier experience of an emotional and physiological arousal that remained unresolved. This could even include unprocessed material belonging to another person to whose emotional state one had attuned to as an infant. All this is exemplified in the story of Rebekah.

I have had people in my experiential courses for professional caregivers where it was clear that they had attuned at a very early age to their mother's emotional state (for example, their mother's body shame) and carried it as an attitude to their own body throughout their life.

We are suggesting that a therapist can open up this area for exploration using the idea of attunement to the affect of the other, their narrative, and also by paying attention to the possibility of a failure of goal-correction within different biological systems within the person. We see the connection between what we are saying and the traditional understanding of transference and its use in therapeutic environments. However, we are expanding the use of the concept to cover not just projected material from the internal environment, but from each of the other six motivational systems as well. In the example given above in relation to shame in relation to one's own body, the origin of this may well have been located in a failure of regulation and goal-correction of the careseeking system many generations deep.

I understood Rebekah's distress through the lens of this model. I had known something of her early childhood, that along with her mother and older sister she had been evacuated from Sri Lanka, or what was then known as Ceylon, in 1942 during the Second World War when the country was afraid of imminent invasion by the Japanese.

The ship, full of women and children, returned to England under escort. It was known to all aboard that the waters in which they travelled contained German submarines and that they were in real danger of being torpedoed at any time. The captain had issued a warning to the mothers on board that if one of their children fell overboard he would not stop as it was too dangerous. They were in a life-threatening situation. While oral history records that the women/mothers made tremendous efforts to keep up their own morale and that of the children, there can be no doubt that the fear surrounding such a journey will have communicated itself to all on board, including the children. And this fear was of an unseen life-threatening force that could attack from underneath with no warning. Such a fear is not easily imagined.

Rebekah told me that it occurred to her that her mother must have told her about the submarines as at three years of age she would have had no such concept, but she wondered whether hearing those words in later life could trigger the same terror. I have no doubt about this as I see this happening all the time in the exploratory groups that I facilitate with professional care-givers. Words can trigger feelings and, if unnoticed or unprocessed by the person, can produce tension in the body. This can mean the feelings them-selves remain unrevealed, unprocessed, and unregulated.

On arrival in the UK Rebekah lived with her mother and her older sister for three years in London until the end of the war, when her mother then returned to her husband in Sri Lanka and placed the two girls in a small boarding school in the south of England.

In the bleakest of boarding schools, Rebekah was separated from her sister; they were in different dormitories and in different classes. Rebekah was completely at the mercy of her own resources to survive. Though not conscious of it, she told me there must have been a moment when she realized the mother she loved was not coming back, was not coming to get her, that she was not going home.

I knew she had used the continuing ticking of her watch as a comforting presence to assure her that she was all right and would survive. What I did not know until we were exploring her history again was that her watch was a present from her parents, and as long as she could hear it ticking she could hear her mother's voice and feel connected. We both realized she was using her watch in the way that Donald Winnicott described the function of a transitional object – an object that carries a significant emotional connection with a person, place or thing (Winnicott, 1958).

Rebekah retained the link with her mother by having the physical presence of her watch. This physical object was therefore a powerful representation of her internal environment, where she was retaining her experience of her mother and father in ways that were supportive of her well-being. Think what might have happened to Rebekah if she had lost the watch or it had been taken from her. I ask the reader to hold this thought in mind for later in the paper as we explore the meaning of the loss of externally supportive objects.

Unfortunately the adults in the school did not provide a safe emotional envir-onment in which feelings of loss or abandonment could have been processed. In fact, Rebekah described the school as a closed system where there were few visits from outsiders, no radio, and no newspapers. She was a lively child and used her natural humour and vivacity to lift the mood of the other children. In the model just outlined she was using humour and distraction as a form of self-defence (self-regulation), a useful strategy but one that promoted self-reliance and self-suffi-ciency in the absence of attuned and supportive caregivers.

While humour could be seen as the outward behaviour of the arousal of her system for self-defence, one can also see how it might be linked with her internal environment. The internal environment is where one logs one's history of inter-actions with others (how people have related to you, what attributions they have made to you or about you, comments that compare you with others or comments about others which are meant to attribute some quality to you by inference. We would also add into this what one has picked up about the other person through attuning to their emotional state and which one then thinks of as an attribute of the self).

In this way we can see how the internal environment can be the place where we retain aspects of significant others which we have attuned to. The capacity to attune to another's emotional state is hard wired into us for survival purposes and happens naturally between mothers and babies. This capacity can, of course, be damaged through life experience relating to the way we have been treated and responded to by others in such a way that influences our genetic organization. It seems to us that we don't give enough credence to the fact that infants and toddlers equally attune to the emotional state of their caregiver and retain those emotions as if they were part of the self, not realizing that they in fact belong to someone else. In addition, it seems plausible that a young child might internalize their 'significant other's' way of managing fear. In other words, they might internalize the other's defensive strategies and use them as part of their own defence resources.

In deflecting the other children from the situation they were in, by using humour and distraction, Rebekah might well have been drawing on her internalized gestalt of how her mother managed her own and her daughters' emotions when in a highly stressed situation. I am thinking here of how Rebekah used humour three or four years later in her boarding school when the other children were distressed and how her mother had used distraction as a way of diverting her daughters' attention from the life-threatening situation they were in on the ship sailing from Sri Lanka. There may be links here that give an eye into how Rebekah was able to keep a living relationship with her mother through what she had internalized from her, albeit not totally within her conscious awareness.

But the job of keeping herself and the other children going was complicated because the women in charge of the school used shame and humiliation as a form of discipline; for instance, a common punishment for some minor misdemeanour was to be made to wear one's school pullover backwards so that the emblem of the school and the V-neck were clearly visible on the back of the child. Not only did the children have to do this within the grounds of the school, but also when they were outside on walks or riding. It was a deeply humiliating experience and one that filled Rebekah with shame.

What is the cost to the self when one's basic survival strategies are themselves attacked and the self is shamed? This has surely got to have a major impact on the internal environment of the person. The question it raises is whether the internal environment as a system within the self is sufficiently robust to support the developing self. The tragedy of this, of course, is that the person carries a sense of themselves (that they are shameful) that has been implanted in them by someone else and has nothing to do with their essential self or how they may actually feel about themselves before they have been made to feel shame.

This fact may also remain occluded from conscious awareness for many years, particularly when (based on my observations in my own practice) the dynamic keeping this situation in place is an attunement with the expression of shame in the embodied person of the other. In other words, when a person shames another they usually have an expression on their face which communicates disgust, hatred or worse. This can leave the person being shamed feeling there is something really hideous inside them; lodging the feelings of shame within the internal organization of the self as if they were part and parcel of the self.

It is not fanciful to think that these experiences with the two women running the school encouraged Rebekah to rely on her own resources and not seek or expect attuned and empathic caregiving from those normally perceived to provide it. It is no surprise that she might have leaned more heavily on her fear system within the biologically based system for self-defence rather than developing and building an effective careseeking system where she could go to others for help.

It was clearly with great resilience that she kept her internal world as supportive as it was (clearly it had unsupportive elements such as vulnerability to feeling shame). This was helped by the presence of her older sister whom she loved, her watch (which linked her to her parents), and her love of and access to animals (the school encouraged horse riding). She had also internalized her mother's love and playful spirit, her Sri Lankan nanny with whom she shared many wonderful experiences of the Sri Lankan countryside, and the magnificent elephants who were part and parcel of everyday life as well as being involved in colourful ceremonial occasions.

This is a glimpse into Rebekah's internal environment, peopled by benign women and wonderful countryside and animals. But, as we have looked at, within that internal environment could have been an attunement to her mother's defensive strategy for coping with terror. In addition there could well have been the vulnerability at the core of the self, mentioned earlier, due to the possible impact of the shaming tactics employed by the adults at the school and other experiences unknown to us. I wonder whether the impact of being shamed can have an effect on the developing systems for sharing interests with peers and sexuality where there is a call on the self for a certain amount of self-exposure?

We have seen how, due to life circumstances, Rebekah's system for protecting herself relied on the more primitive fear system, particularly if aroused in circumstances where she was all alone in the world, with no family present and no benign, capable, effective adults around.

To return to Rebekah's story. For many years, while Rebekah and her sister attended this school, they spent all the school vacations with various families. As one can imagine, this was a less than satisfactory situation. After three years in this boarding school they were visited by their parents, who spent an extended leave in the UK. On their parents' return journey to Sri Lanka they made friends with an elderly couple who were about to retire to England. They explained to the couple their distress at leaving their two daughters and an understanding was reached with this couple that they would assume guardianship of the girls once they retired to the south of England. The couple had no children of their own and there was an age difference of about 20 years between the man and the woman – the man being older. They agreed to look after the girls during all school holidays and to take on the job of guardianship in the absence of their parents.

Although this arrangement took some time to get established, Rebekah finally bonded with this couple and felt safe and secure in their family. The couple had three cocker spaniels and a poodle, all four dogs making excellent emotional bridges particularly between Rebekah and the two adults.

The sisters settled into their new family and their beautiful country home. From there on they spent all school holidays with this couple and eventually left school and went to university. But by this stage both considered this couple and their home as part and parcel of their life and times. While the couple kept very clear boundaries that they were not the children's parents, nevertheless strong affectional bonds were formed on all sides and the two girls growing up got advice and support as they launched themselves into adult life. The younger, Rebekah, worked in London and was able to return to her guardians' home every weekend. The bond deepened as Rebekah took root in the very soil of the garden as well as the love and affection she felt for the couple.

The journey that I referred to at the beginning of the chapter took place several years later. At this point the couple, particularly the man who, as said earlier, was twenty years older than his wife, decided for practical financial reasons to downsize, sell their beautiful home, and move to a smaller place where there was just one bedroom and a small dressing room; in other words, there was no designated bedroom for Rebekah.

Rebekah lost her home. Naturally she was devastated. This was the second-time round, and while she may well have had the feelings that she had experienced as a young child when alone in her boarding school when she finally realized her mother was not coming back and she was on her own, she was unlikely to be aware of the earlier roots to her present despair. In fact, she was not aware at that time that there might be a connection. It was only recently, when working in session with me, that an intimation of these connections struck home and made such a difference

At the time this was happening, Rebekah was aware of losing the house and grounds where she had lived and loved. Her immediate thought was to take out a mortgage on the property, which would have maintained the status quo. She could have afforded to do this. And the idea to do this emerged naturally out of her experience that this was her home and her family. However, this was not discussed between herself and the couple: the idea could not be entertained. After all, she was not family. It was at this moment that Rebekah left the house in anger to embark on the journey north to take up post-graduate study. Some hours later she lost her way on the road and was totally distraught. Distraught, though, is not a big enough word; the experience felt traumatic. It *was* traumatic and it has lasted a lifetime.

Rebekah explained to me that it was like losing all one's senses, her body went into a state of deep shock, and when she recovered herself she was white and frozen. Slowly she began to find her coordinates. But for the timeline that her experience of terror lasted she experienced, in her own words, 'the nearest thing ever to being completely destroyed'.

This was a deeply biological state, a state akin to what Donald Winnicott has called a 'breakdown' (see his excellent paper, 'Fear of Breakdown' (Winnicott, 1974), which describes the breakdown we fear as a breakdown that we have already experienced). It was a state of such severe sensory disorganization that Rebekah quite naturally has no desire to re-experience it. Her analyst had described it as a 'fugue' state. Rebekah had never found this helpful as she felt it labelled her in a medical way and failed to help her understand her experience.

I heard what she was talking about with a completely different ear. I heard it through the lens of Rebekah's personally created external environment – i. e., her home – on which there had been a major assault. I placed it in the context of her earlier history of losing her original home in Sri Lanka, the terrifying journey to the UK, and then later losing her home in London when her mother returned to Sri Lanka and placed her in a boarding school, not to be visited for a further three years.

Creating a personally supportive external environment comes from an instinctive motivational system within all of us that is guided by an internal template of what we have experienced as supportive in the past. The conceptual basis of this system could be seen as akin to Winnicott's idea of a 'transitional object' based on his observations of children and their intense emotional attachment to objects such as teddy bears, pieces of cloth, etc.

Heard and Lake, in my view, have extended Winnicott's observation of the child's tie to an object and located it within a separate biological system which they call the personally created external environment (PCEE). This system evolves throughout a lifetime and is not only confined to childhood. The personally created external environment is the lifestyle which reminds a person of where the goals of the five aspects of the self have been met to the highest degree so far experienced (Heard, Lake & McCluskey, 2012, p. 117).

Rebekah's story illustrates the way a transitional object can be used in Winnicottian terms; that is, to retain a link with a meaningful person – remember the significance of the watch. Winnicott's idea forms part of our understanding of the system for personally creating a supportive or unsupportive external environment. The significance of an external environment that we create ourselves is different for each one of us.

I wonder if the importance we give to it can sometimes be linked to our survival. What has enabled us to survive absence and loss of significant people, culture, homeland, class, and position in our lives (such as the example of Rebekah)? How we construct our environment is clearly linked to resources, circumstances, and also what importance we attach to it in terms of its function in our overall well-being.

If the functioning of this system is interrupted, prevented from reaching its goal or destroyed by war, poverty or neglect, the impact on the person and sometimes generations to follow is something we are only beginning to understand.

This is a description of the biological system (PCEE). However, underneath the assault on this system in Rebekah's case (as would be the case for anyone else) lay meaningful connections with past internalized events. Other biological systems within Rebekah were going to be affected by this state of affairs (given that all seven systems work as a single process), but to the fore, as Rebekah realizes, is likely to be the arousal of the system for self-defence. This system will be informed by the internal environment: 'lookalikes' to the past will be tracked through and found (at a level outside consciousness) and a defensive organization searched for (again at a speed outside conscious awareness: see Bowlby (1988) and Heard, Lake and McCluskey (2009) for an elaboration of the system for self-defence and the mechanisms by which events and experiences are excluded from consciousness) to manage the present turmoil. What Rebekah was conveying, I think, was that at this moment no such defensive organization or strategy was available to her; she was rudderless and totally at risk. The 'lookalike' to the past one imagines might well be that horrifying time when she made the journey from her secure and happy home in Sri Lanka to England in the company of adults and children who had no certainty they would survive.

Let us examine the evidence for this particular understanding from the point of view of rupture within the system of the personally created external environment. At its most simple, Rebekah lost her home. She lost her security and her assumptions and aspirations about her future. She lost her creative space. The garden and the general ambience of the house and the countryside it was located in provided Rebekah with what Henry James might describe as the 'requirements of her aesthetic imagination'. It did more than that; it is likely that it found resonance within her to the orderly beauty of her early home in Sri Lanka and memories of being out in the open in sunshine with people she loved and felt secure with.

While she did not design or create the interior of the house or that of the garden, she was sufficiently invested in their transformation and development to consider them her own project. And the whole project gave her much satisfaction and pleasure. Other systems within the attachment dynamic were also assuaged by this arrangement. Her interest sharing system, her caregiving system, and her system for seeking care. She got good emotional and intellectual support from the couple, particularly the woman who was highly intelligent and resourceful. In addition it was a place to heal some of the earlier traumas of the past and continue her development as a person.

The decision of her guardians to sell, and the decision not to consult Rebekah or accept financial help from her, brutally clarified that the couple did not see her as they might a daughter with having 'rights' to what happened to her 'home'. In one stroke she had again 'lost' her 'parents' and lost her home.

Her biological need to have a home which holds and contains objects and symbols and all the good supportive experiences of one's life was being destroyed for a second time. I put this view to Rebekah and she was immediately relieved. She had never seen it like this. The process of this work has triggered new insights and connections for her. One of the most powerful was when she remembered that what had happened to her as a child had also happened to her mother.

Her maternal grandmother and grandfather emigrated to Canada from the UK and started their family out there. They set about farming. But her maternal grandfather was killed by the kick of an animal, leaving his widow alone with three children. There was nothing for it but for his widow to return to the UK with her children. She made a hazardous journey across the land mass of Canada and then rough passage on the seas on her way back home. She had no money, she was ill with TB, and she had the care of three children under the age of seven (Rebekah's mother was the middle child, aged about five). She headed for her husband's family in Scotland. Her Scottish relatives could not cope, they were experiencing famine themselves, and sent her away. She went to Cornwall, where her own family came from. As she remembered this incident in her mother's early life, Rebekah got a sense that the power of the dynamic may well have been compounded by the fact that there were two generations of unprocessed trauma at play.

This book is about how we can understand more fully what our clients are communicating to us by listening out for the way in which instinctive motivational systems have been activated within the person but where they have failed to reach their goal. The failure of these biological systems to reach their goal has a massive effect on the well-being of the person. The one we have just been looking at is the personally created external environment. In my experience this aspect of a person's life is often overlooked and certainly not understood from an evolutionary and attachment perspective. I have found that the personally created external environment is one of the most important systems for enabling well-being and promoting creativity.

Summary

This chapter explored the way in which a person was enabled to overcome an earlier traumatic experience that was multi-layered and multi-generational. The trauma was embedded in the body and was experienced as an acute state of shock accompanied by a terrifying sensation of not being able to hold it together, of losing one's senses.

The meaning of this experience was explored from the point of view of biologically based goal-corrected systems. This suggests that the person remains affected in ways that may be outside their consciousness until the system that has been aroused finally achieves its goal. In the personal story explored in this chapter, the traumatic experience was linked to the loss of a personally created external environment and the way that environment had supported crucial aspects of the self. While it was sufficient in this case to make a meaningful connection between the feelings of terror and the loss of Rebekah's supportive environment, our work together surfaced other connections. Rebekah herself posits that the physical shock she experienced in the car on her journey north that day was linked directly with the state of terror she experienced on the ship back to England, when it and its crew sailed in very hostile and threatening waters – hard, in those circumstances, as a three-year-old to create an externally supportive environment. The fear was contained in her body, ready to be aroused when a 'lookalike' in the present showed itself.

The interdependence of the seven biological systems was also explored in terms of how they affected the functioning of one another. So, for instance, the internal environment was both supportive of the self but also unsupportive, especially where it might be called on to support the systems of interest sharing with peers and sexuality to reach their goal. One could see how careseeking was inhibited by the experience of the loss of the original caregiver and subsequent experience of non-attunement and total lack of empathy by the owners and managers of the boarding school. Clearly the story is much more nuanced and complex than presented here, but I am grateful to Rebekah, now in her late seventies and thriving, for engaging with this as a joint project. Her story certainly illuminates how one can locate the nature of the trauma being presented as having a connection with a key system in the dynamic organization of the person.

The point being made in this chapter is that it was crucial that the professional caregiver understood that the aspect of the self being presented for attention by Rebekah was the threat to her personally created external environment. Rebekah didn't know she was presenting this; she was expressing her terror and paralysis and her lack of understanding about the nature of this experience. But she experienced the relief one normally experiences when the careseeking self reaches its goal. This indicated to her and her caregiver that they had unravelled the nature of her distress. The theory being presented here (Ainsworth et al., 1977; Heard & Lake, 1997; McCluskey, 2005) suggests that when careseeking reaches its goal the person returns to their normal exploratory self. This is clearly what happened in this case, and Rebekah and her caregiver went on to unearth many more dimensions and meanings behind the initial presentation which has given much relief, connection, and satisfaction to Rebekah. The evidence for transformation is that she is now travelling and meeting her friends.

In the next two chapters we explore how the defensive self can act as the keystone system for the person and how this can be worked with within this model to enable the person to begin to access their careseeking self in a straightforward way and risk relating from that part of themselves. In Chapter Four we have the account from the professional caregiver's point of view, while in Chapter Five we hear from the careseeker.

Chapter 4

One's affectionate careseeking self

The keystone system as the source of the transference

In this chapter we consider the way we think about transference and how it influences our work. We explore how a therapist can locate transferential phenomena within each of the seven different systems located within the attachment dynamic as identified by Heard and Lake. O'Toole outlines his work with a client, whom he calls Jean, who attended therapy with him on a weekly basis, sometimes twice weekly, for almost ten years, and gives a unique insight into how this theory can work in practice. He charts the various stages of the work, culminating in what Jean called the 'hardest and most difficult piece of the work', which was the transference between the therapist and client. The transference was understood using the map offered by Heard and Lake which details the various biological systems operating within the self of the therapist (or professional caregiver) and the self of the client (careseeker).

In this case the careseeking aspect of Jean was seen as the source of the transference. However, each of the other systems within could be seen as interconnected and interrelated. When people are distressed and approach a caregiver/therapist for help, they communicate both consciously and unconsciously the nature of what is upsetting them. From an attachment perspective we consider that distress and dysfunction can emanate from aspects of the self that have become aroused but may be unknown to the person. It is this new perspective we bring to the work.

What became clear from O'Toole's work was how vulnerable a person can feel when approaching someone else for help, especially when one's experience has been of nobody ever being there, of being left behind. Of course, we all know this, but it is exactly this vulnerability that arouses other aspects of the self that makes it difficult for change to happen. The vulnerability has to be addressed in all the various ways to enable a person to enter the arena of exploratory work. This can only be done through the caregiver remaining undefensive themselves and able to attune and empathize with the state of the other in such a way as they feel safe, secure, and understood.

This case demonstrated what happens to the self when we don't experience what it means 'to be met as a person'. The theory being put forward here is a map and a guide which informs us that, until the goal of the careseeking system is reached through a particular interaction with an empathic and responsive caregiver, this system will remain active, albeit in defence mode seeking resolution, until it reaches its goal.

The job of the caregiver is to respond to the unmet careseeking need and to notice how the person seeking care is communicating this need in disguised form. Whatever form the behaviour takes, the system of careseeking will remain active and unassuaged until it receives the right and appropriate response. Until this response is effective and embodied by the person seeking care, their fear system will be on high alert, active and vigilant to any real or potential threat or danger, especially in the context of seeking care or help from another person.

What the careseeker requires is someone who will be able to remain in exploratory mode, to help them to feel safe enough to experience inside themselves their own internal self at a biological cellular level. The caregiver needs to be able to help the person seeking care to access the information inside their own bodies, to express this information in an embodied form. It may require the caregiver working with the careseeker to keep their feet on the ground, remain fully centred in their emotion, and making good and appropriate eye contact with their caregiver. This intervention by the professional caregiver, which could be seen as dictatorial, comes from a very profound sense of calling the other into a relationship with them so that the meaning of both emotion and body experiences can be explored. But this intervention goes along in parallel to working with the client to engage and access their curiosity about themselves so that they are not simply submitting to the wishes of the caregiver.

As professional caregivers it is easy to forget how vulnerable it is to look for care from another human being, to trust another person with what we know about ourselves but cannot share. We are frightened that if we share that vulnerable part we will not survive. For this reason, our system for self-defence takes over. It protects us from the fear of what might happen, the breakdown we already have had, as Winnicott talks about in his paper 'Fear of Breakdown' (Winnicott, 1974). We are asking clients to put their system for self-defence to one side for long enough to 'stand in the spaces', as Bromberg (1998) says, so that the careseeking system can be met in all its vulnerability. If this can happen slowly, and with sufficient patience and care on the part of the caregiver, something new is possible, a new breath can be taken, a new step made, a new person can be experienced and allowed to stand with them.

We have given this book the subtitle 'A Guide for Professional Caregivers', and having a guide is enormously helpful and supportive. But it is something that takes a backseat when we are with the person sitting in front of us. As Seamus Heaney says of the process of writing poetry, 'The movement is from delight to wisdom and not vice versa' (Heaney, 1995, p. 4).

When Jean sat down with me on that first day, neither of us knew what would unfold. We had to learn how to be together in a way that allowed a process to unfold. This process would rub up against both our histories and demand more of both of us than we knew was possible at that early stage. Jean entered my room on that first day a very frightened, insecure, terrified woman who thought I would have all the answers and that I would fix her because of my professional status and knowledge. She had no sense that she would need to meet me as a person, and I would have to find a way to meet her if she was to find a way forward.

This is a common perception of many people who come for help. They have no awareness of having to enter a new space, like having to enter a new building, and to enter a relationship. This is not something in their conscious awareness, that it will be asked of them. This is why the concept of a secure base, which was introduced into attachment theory by Ainsworth (1978), is so important. Ainsworth got the idea of a secure base from her student days through the work of one of her lecturers, by the name of Blatz, who had the hypothesis that 'infants (once they were mobile) would explore the world around them, but only so long as they felt they were in touch with a secure base, to which they could return at any time' (Heard, Lake & McCluskey, 2009, p. 229).

Establishing a secure base with a person seeking help is the foundation of any further exploration in psychotherapy. Holmes, in the preface to his book 'Exploring in Security', suggests that 'The book title reflects one of the simple, yet profound ideas attachment has brought to our discipline: the mutual incompatibility of insecurity and exploration. This leads to the paradox whose unravelling is central to the business of psychotherapy, that until safety prevails, careseeking people – i.e. a "patient" or "client" – cannot begin to explore themselves, their life situation, and their feelings; yet it is that very insecurity that brings them for help' (Holmes, 2010, Preface). Holmes goes on to suggest that 'The task of therapy is both to *explore insecurity*, its origins and ramifications, and to provide a space where a person can *explore in security*' (Holmes, 2010, Preface). I will now outline the case of Jean and the work that followed using the theory presented here.

Phase one: establishing a secure base

Jean made contact with O'Toole in the late summer of 2009 due to a number of difficulties in her life. He will now continue the narrative in the first person singular. She was referred to me by her GP as she was feeling anxious and had very little support in her life. She was then in her early forties, single, with no family of her own. She lived alone and felt very isolated in her life. She had not been in a romantic or intimate relationship since her early twenties and felt she was a failure because of this. Her internal environment was very critical and she had a very rigid form of thinking. She described having a very conflictual relationship with her mother. Jean grew up with both parents but there was constant tension and rows in the home. Her parents were controlling, had quick tempers, and would lash out verbally and physically towards each other and the children. When Jean was fourteen years old she decided she could not fight back anymore and instead, when she was involved in a row, she would withdraw and stop talking for days. Her parents separated when she was seventeen. She never spoke to her father again, he never made contact with her, and she would cross the road to make sure her father didn't see her. Her father died ten years prior to the point of her referral and her mother had remarried. Jean lives close to many of her siblings, with whom she has a good relationship.

My first contact with Jean was when she phoned me for an appointment. I arranged to meet with her and on the day of the appointment, as I waited in my office, Jean phoned to check if I was ready to see her. I thought this was an unusual request. However, it was something I was to get used to over the next ten years of our work together. Jean continues to phone me to check if I am available to see her, if I have forgotten her, or if I am with someone more important. Establishing a secure base with Jean meant seeing this behaviour as a form of careseeking and not as controlling. Mary Main's work with 'children who are deemed disorganised/disoriented with mother in infancy showed controlling, role inverting behaviour and were either punitive and directive or solicitous and caregiving' (Main & Cassidy, 1988). 'These children were respectively termed controlling-punitive and controlling-caregiving' (Main, 1995, p. 433). Main goes on to suggest that children who were 'disorganised as infants attempt, in part, to "solve" the "irresolvable" paradox presented by the frightened/frightening attachment figure by stepping into the role of the caregiver' (Main, 1995, p. 433).

In our model we see this behaviour as careseeking, which is being overridden by the fear aspect of the system for self-defence. Jean's defensive self is triggered by the idea of making contact with me, and her behaviour is disconnected from the arousal of her careseeking self. This is partly fuelled by her need to protect herself from the possible rejection she might face if her careseeking is not met by a welcoming and available caregiver. Whatever way this dynamic has developed with a person, the process is already well established before they enter the room. In Jean's case I am curious about the phone call and the need to check if I am available, but by remaining curious, rather than getting annoyed or defensive, I am in a better position to understand and process the behaviour. By checking to see if I am available, Jean's careseeking self is being infiltrated by her defensive self and possibly by a very unsupportive internal environment. 'In her Charlottesville study, Cassidy (1988) found that controlling children tended to have a concept of the self as negative and bad' (Main, 1995, p. 434).

After the initial appointment Jean did not wish to make a follow-up appointment. I forgot about Jean until I heard from her again after a month, when she phoned me requesting another appointment. I had been 'good-enough'. Again, my phone rang while I waited in my office; it was Jean checking to see if I was available to see her. We continued to meet over the next ten years every week and sometimes twice a week.

Phase two: shall I or shall I not have a baby?

The issue of wanting to have a baby dominated our work in the first two years. This was an extremely difficult time for Jean as she struggled to decide if this was what she desired and whether she was able or willing to go ahead with the idea of having a baby on her own. She had felt a failure for not having found a partner and not having had a family of her own. She felt it was her fault and that her situation would never change. Her internal environment was vicious as she lashed out at herself for being a failure. She was putting all of her energy into trying to decide whether to go ahead or not with the baby. Afraid to let go and afraid to go ahead, she oscillated between these two poles of what seemed like her very existence. She was tormented. She thought I would be able to tell her what to do. Jean said, 'I always wanted children, and when the reality hit that I would not become a mother I questioned my very being, I mourned the life I would never have, and I grieved for the children I would never see'.

At this point Jean's energy was very frantic, which she burned with continuous activity, cleaning the house, exercising, working conscientiously, terrified of making a mistake.

Phase three: Jean's activity level as a form of self-regulation

Jean's high level of activity soon became evident in her behaviour in the sessions, where she spoke very rapidly. Her words sometimes were not able to keep up with how fast her brain was working. From years spent in the barren wilderness of her life, Jean's internal world poured out into the sessions which became her lifeline. In this drawing she illustrates something of that inner world that exploded onto the stage of our weekly meetings.

The explosion of figures and the amount of movement illustrate much more vividly than words can describe her experience of being able to let out all her pent-up anger, frustration, disappointment, sadness, loss, envy, desolation, aloneness. They show both a depth and breadth of experience being given life and expression in this new space where she was able to enter and come into connection with another person for the first time in her life. They also contrast painfully with the absence of any intimate relating which, Jean described, characterized the rest of her life outside of her sessions.

Figure 4.1 Reproduced from 'A combined approach to psychotherapy, individual and group, from an attachment perspective', Attachment Journal, 10: 2 (October 2016), p. 123.

Phase four: Jean engages in individual and group therapy based on this model of working

The fourth phase of our work together happened after Jean had been in individual therapy with me for over four years. At this point I was putting together a group based on the McCluskey model of working with the dynamics of attachment in adult life. I had a number of people who had been in individual therapy with me for some time who I thought would benefit from a group experience in parallel with their individual session (see O'Toole, 2016).

I invited Jean to be part of this group intervention. Jean experienced this invitation as very threatening and we spent six months negotiating her transition to the group process. This was a really important part of building and deepening Jean's trust in me. Her fear escalated at the thought of people knowing who she was or of meeting someone she knew. She was afraid that I was abandoning her; was I sick of listening to her? she asked. We agreed that she would come early on the first night and could scan the faces of the people who came to the group, and that she could leave immediately if she knew someone. She did not phone me to check if I was available or ready to meet her when she came to the group. I ran the group on a monthly basis with each individual participant continuing in individual weekly psychotherapy. This was also an essential part in supporting

Jean in dealing with her experience of working in a group with other people. It also led to a deepening of her individual work.

Jean's defensive self

Jean experienced a lot of anger with a man in the group during the session exploring the system on self-defence. This was an expression of Jean's fear system in full force. She was terrified of the force of her anger that she was experiencing within herself, and at one point she stormed out of the session. She returned after a few minutes and said, 'I am here to learn'. I stopped her expressing her anger to the man, which in turn made her very angry with me. She said in her individual session she did not think I would be able 'to take her on', meaning I would not be able to face and tolerate her rage. This work on the self-defence system was very scary for Jean and only through many intense individual sessions was she able to work with her level of anger and fear.

However, when the time came for starting a second round of the group experience to explore the seven systems, Jean was happy to participate. Jean felt that she wouldn't get as much from doing the group the second time, but, as she said herself, 'I was wrong'. It was a question raised by a new member that provided clarity around careseeking and self-defence for her. 'I felt I got it!' she said. The validation from feeling she understood that the system for self-defence is a response to failed careseeking was evident in her joy. 'I felt I got it.' We refer readers to O'Toole's (2016) paper for a more detailed discussion of how this model can be effectively explored through group therapy, which is also supported by individual work with the same therapist.

Phase five: Jean's interest sharing self

In the second year of the combined group and individual work, Jean dropped down into the emptiness of her life during the session where the group was exploring their interest sharing selves. While the others in the group explored their interests, Jean felt the familiar feeling of being left behind. She explored this live in the group as her trust in the group had deepened and, as she said, 'she did not want to bring it home with her'.

She explored what it felt like to be left behind and the sadness she felt. She had caught hold of something in the experience of being a participant in the group while also feeling alone. Jean brought this work into her individual therapy at our next appointment. After the group experience, she had drawn a picture to capture her individual experience.

In the session with me she began by saying she had no words and could not move, but she wanted to show me what she had got hold of since the group session. She asked if she could walk around the room and if I would accompany her. She said 'this is it…'. She could visualize the space and she said 'this is where I felt left as a child, I had no words, I couldn't talk. It wasn't all bad, but it was sad'.

Figure 4.2 Reproduced from 'A combined approach to psychotherapy, individual and group, from an attachment perspective', Attachment Journal, 10: 2 (October 2016), p. 127.

In the diagram, she has drawn a small child in the corner of the picture enveloped in her own world. The diagram depicts how she grew from this place in the corner, where she had no words and could not move, through a series of images of herself until she emerges as a fully grown adult where she is in contact with me (the tall figure on the right), who is both looking back at her as an infant and forward to her as the adult. There is a light cord connecting each of the figures in the drawing. This drawing reminds me of Sonntag's work with her patient 'Olivia' when Olivia says, 'Words just don't cut it' (Sonntag, 2006, p. 330).

Phase six: careseeking system as the source of the transference presented through the affectionate sexual system

I did not realize the full significance of the above drawing and its connection with the next piece of work until I discussed it with McCluskey in preparing this chapter. As already stated, Jean's primary defence is one of fight and flight. She has remained out of connection to herself or to anyone else for most of her adult life. Her interactions are dominated by fear – fear of judgment, fear of abandonment, fear of intimacy.

It is even difficult at this point to convey the pain of the dynamics at work at the core of Jean's personality and how they are played out in her life, in particular in her transferential connection with me as her caregiver. She feels rejection everywhere in her life. She checks all the time that she is playing by the rules and does not overstay her allotted time. This behaviour of checking masks her desperate need to belong, to feel welcome, not to have to get up and leave. A lifetime of failed careseeking leaves the person in a constant state of alert.

The piece of work I wish to focus on here is when Jean asked me if she could hold my hand during one of our sessions. Like the phone calls, I was aware that this was an unusual request and, as a male therapist, I was very aware of how vulnerable a position I was being put in. I was also aware of how big it was for her to ask to hold my hand. I knew this request was coming from a very young part of Jean and it felt important not to refuse such a request. Jean had spoken previously about having many issues with her skin, especially her hands, which would break out into a rash when she was young, particularly in times of stress. She also spoke about how her father would hold his hand in front of her face and threaten her.

I was also aware that I did not have any countertransference feeling of sexual attraction for Jean and was as sure as I could be that this was also true for Jean. She had said she did not have feelings for me, but this was a request to hold my hand. I knew my client's fear of rejection was very strong, and I did not want to reject her in any way. However, I was unaware of the intensity of her feelings of rejection, and, more importantly, I was not aware of how her fear of rejection was masking her real need to connect and the intensity of that need. This only became clear to me as the work progressed. Having discussed this with McCluskey I now see this piece of the work as Jean's careseeking system being trumped by the very young affectionate sexual system of which the careseeking/caregiving relationship is a template for the adult form. In the absence of her careseeking needs being met as an infant or child, each of the different aspects of Jean's self was used defensively to mask her careseeking self. In this way Jean had no way of communicating the many different behaviours of each of the different systems within the self through various stages of the work. This aspect of the self, because of its vulnerability and the risk of shame and rejection it entailed, could only be exposed after an enormous amount of trust was built up in our work together.

Perhaps the biggest lesson for me in this piece of work with Jean was that the intensity of the need that the person is defending against experiencing (internally) is matched by the opposite presentation in the relationship with the other person (externally). For example, my experience of Jean was that she held me at a distance (remember the phone calls before every session). I was unaware that this shielded a desire for intimacy. Having an awareness of this dynamic relationship between the need and the defence that lies in front of the need has been enormously helpful to me as a psychotherapist, and something that my work with Jean has taught me. Both parties learn and are changed by the interaction.

In order to allow Jean to hold my hand, I moved my chair alongside her chair. Jean explored what it felt like to hold my hand and talked about feeling closer to me and being able to connect with herself in a new way. She felt safe in herself, in a way that she felt she could not through words alone. She felt safe enough to drop her guard of having to do everything for herself all the time. She was always clear to ask if it was okay to hold my hand and she always made a point of saying that she did not have feelings for me. By this she meant that she did not have sexual feelings for me.

I was aware of being put in a position where it was not easy for me to refuse to allow Jean to hold my hand without rejecting her. But what was this action preventing? I was also aware of feeling restricted, in the sense that I felt I could no longer refuse my client permission to hold my hand without rejecting her. But, of course, this was what she was enacting. This was the 'wished for' object relationship. 'Through getting the analyst to enact with the patient, the latter achieves a measure of reality for his or her transference fantasies. Enactments occur when an attempt to actualize a transference fantasy elicits a counter-transference reaction' (Chused, 1986, p. 102).

I allowed Jean to hold my hand three times. Then on the fourth occasion, after Jean asked to hold my hand, I knew I had to address this request. I said we needed to talk about her holding my hand. It was my job as the caregiver to address the shift from a transference need or wish to an enactment in a way that tried to help my client move from an early non-verbal form of careseeking to a more mature verbal form of careseeking, where the want and need can be verbalized safely even if not gratified. In order to do this I had to emphasize to Jean that her need to hold my hand was not wrong. But how she was asking to have this need met had to be explored therapeutically.

I was asking Jean to make the shift from acting out an archaic need to be held, to verbalize this need. And not only that, but to experience the pain of rejection she felt in the core of her body because this need was never met as a child by her primary carers and hence this need was experienced by her in her internal environment as wrong in the first place. Her internal representation of her experience of relationships was that she could only get what she wanted from the other person on their terms. Beginning to explore what is behind the verbal request of wanting to hold my hand was a very fragile process and was felt as dangerous by both careseeker and caregiver.

As soon as I said we needed to talk about holding my hand I saw Jean withdraw into a very terrified state in front of me. She was withdrawing to a place deep inside herself where she is almost beyond reach. All I could see was six years of work going down the drain. I kept reminding her not to make the need wrong. That it was necessary to explore how she was getting the need met. I was aware that she was no longer seeing or hearing me. All she wanted was to leave the room and not come back. I knew I had to stay very connected to her and to stay really steady. This was new territory for both of us.

Jean's enactment was a defence against the whole restorative process which required her to experience the pain of rejection and loss in order to be able to experience 'a new beginning' (Balint, 1952). This shift from enactment to verbali-zation enabled a development in all of the different systems within the self. But the keystone system that was arrested because of a continuous failure on the part of her primary attachment figures to provide effective goal-corrected empathic caregiving resulted in the goal of careseeking not being met in Jean's life. This very early form of careseeking absolutely requires an attuned empathic response from another person; the person cannot reach the goal of careseeking on their own and it is careseeking at the embodied preverbal level.

My response was 'good enough'. Jean stayed in the room for the session, and for the next session, and the one after that. She came back to the theme of rejection over and over again. She described how she felt alone again and felt right back at the start of our work. She felt she was put in her box. She felt like giving up.

She realized that she was the one who needed to come forward this time. When she first came for help, she saw me as the expert who was going to provide all the answers and to make her life better. All she would have to do was submit to my authority and she would be saved. We all know it is not that easy. This accurately aligns with her internal narrative of relationship, that she can only get what she needs by submission to the authority and dominance of the other person, especially the male. She explored every detail of the experience she felt at the moment I raised the issue with her of holding my hand. We spent up to a year on what it was like for her to feel the level of rejection she experienced in her body at that moment. We worked through her emotions in a new way. Jean learned that she could no longer rely on an infantile mode of relating through touch alone. She had to learn a new language for how she felt and to relate as a separate human being. She had never known how to be separate and connected at the same time. Her only experience of separateness was isolation, and her only experience of connection was a loss of self or engulfment.

Jean spoke about how she always played by the rules but even still she gets it wrong. She felt she had overstepped the boundary and had been put back in her box by me. She could see that, before this time, when she felt hurt and rejected she would always walk away, 'never let them see they hurt you'. But this time she stayed and spoke of the hurt and pain she felt. She was able to say 'you hurt me'. She was also angry that I had rejected her. But first she had to blame herself. She could not risk negotiating with the other person until she felt safe enough to say 'you hurt me' and I did not reject her for this. She no longer experienced me as rejecting of her or angry with her. She was able to see a kind face that cared for her.

Jean was able to say she missed holding my hand, and she feels she has to do everything by herself. Up to now Jean could not countenance connection without being beside the other, holding hands or joined at the hip. It was terrifying for her to let go and face losing the only chance she saw to ever be 'met as a person'.

Jean knows we are coming to the end of our work together and she wants to be able to stay long enough to feel ready to leave in a secure place. I have challenged her that she now needs to relate to me as an adult woman. This is a big challenge for her but she is responding to it. She had gone back to college, which is giving her more opportunities to develop friendships and engage with her peers. She is redecorating her house to build a more supportive external environment, and to support her moving into a new phase in her work life. She is able to recognize when she gets anxious and to regulate her anxiety by reality checking and careseeking from other people in her family. She can now recognize that her family of many brothers, sisters, nieces, and nephews are her family, and this is where she belongs – not as the child she once was, but as the adult woman she now is. Her energy levels and vitality are returning to a new level. She says, 'I have a sense of space now, where I can walk about and look around. I'm living in myself'.

Reflection

This person's core psychological organization was based on a highly active system for self-defence, particularly in the interpersonal realm. Her 'careseeking self' was reduced to the non-verbal symbolic enactment level. Her system for self-defence was dominated by the fear aspect manifested in the fight and flight mode of defending herself in the face of a threat, which could be experienced by the other as controlling. Jean's whole psychological development was affected by her unresolved careseeking self; and when she began to feel the relief when this aspect of the self was met, other aspects of herself came to the fore and flourished as described.

In the next chapter I return to Jean's story, where she gives her own account of what happened to her at the moment when I said 'we need to talk about holding my hand'. This will give the reader a detailed insight into the way the self remains present, even though biologically based interacting systems are acting in ways that might be inhibiting the development of the person.

Postscript

I had not read Patrick Casement's (1982) paper – 'Some pressures on the analyst for physical contact during the reliving of an early trauma' – until after I had completed the work on this chapter. However, I think it would be an omission not to refer to it.

The issue of being asked to hold a patient's hand is central to the case presented by Casement and is not often addressed in the literature. In the beginning of his paper, Casement asks the question:

Is physical contact with the patient, even of a token kind, always to be precluded without question under the classical rule of abstinence? Or are there some occasions when this might be appropriate, even necessary as Margaret Little has suggested in relation to episodes of delusional transference or as Balint and Winnicott have illustrated in relation to periods of deep repression?

(Casement, 1982, p. 279)

I will not go into the full details of the case presented by Casement, but refer the reader to his own account of what occurred between him and his patient after the initial offer to hold the patient's hand was made and was subsequently withdrawn by the therapist. As Casement puts it:

> Contrary to what some people have assumed, my decision to withdraw the offer of my hand was not in any way made on the basis of any rule of abstinence. It was based on following the patient at a deeper level than just that of her surface communications to me ... And when we do follow the patient's communications beyond just the manifest level of what is being asked of us, or demanded, we sometimes arrive at a position that is far less comfortable than anything we might have personally have chosen.
>
> (Casement, 2002, p. 88)

Given the similarities and the differences (as all cases are different and unique) between the two cases, I am of the view that, while the decisions in relation to holding the patient's hand were different, the decisions were made on similar grounds and for similar reasons, to support the development of the autonomy of the person seeking our help.

Chapter 5

One's defensive self

The keystone system as the source of the transference

In this chapter we return to Jean's account of what happened for her when O'Toole said 'We need to talk about you wanting to hold my hand', in order to explore the nature of the system for self-defence as the source of the transference. Jean's account gives a unique insight into the client's experience and her understanding of her system for self-defence, in full force, as it was happening contemporaneously with the clinical intervention. We look at the caregiver's responses, which facilitated the work to move from enactment to verbalization and offered Jean a safe passage from her defensive self to her careseeking self.

Jean wrote the following account immediately after the session where O'Toole said 'We need to talk about you wanting to hold my hand'. O'Toole did not have access to this material until recently, when he had discussed the possibility of writing about this piece of work for publication. These are Jean's words written in a sort of poetry verse style. It is rare to have a careseeker's account of what happens when one goes into a very terrified state within the careseeking/caregiving therapeutic dynamic. She begins…

> Then it started
>
> He started to speak to me
>
> At first, I wasn't sure what he was saying.
>
> The more he spoke the more it hurt
>
> My physical reaction was the first responder and took over
>
> My muscles all tensed up
>
> I could see him, I could hear him,
>
> My body was reacting
>
> As he spoke the feelings got worse, went deeper,
>
> Down to my core

To the depths of me

I was fixed to the chair

No muscles were moving

Except my heart to breathe, very quietly,

My eyes were the only portal to the world.

To the root of the pain.

My head was bursting with all the tension

I didn't move.

I stared intently at this person in shock at what he was saying

Frozen

My breathing slowed to a minimal

Survival mode, very quiet and slow

I was on high alert, yet hearing

I was being hurt

I was ready to make a move

I was being held captive inside

Protecting myself from this perceived threat

I watched him intently

I watched his every move

My sensory perception of him was on high alert

If he made a move, I was gone

I watched him, he remained seated

I notice a slight movement

He has moved the position of his left foot

He is leaning towards me

Speaking in a low, calm voice

He is not posing a threat

His eyes are soft and match his words

I heard him say 'you have done nothing wrong'

He didn't stop talking, he kept talking

I can see his hands move

I still see them. He is explaining what he needs to explain

I am silent

My muscles tightly gripped inside

I am sinking

My eyes fill with tears

It is so painful

Still he talks

My eyes are playing a double role

One of instinct and protection

The other trying to believe what I am actually seeing

My ears listen, they are engaged

My brain is beginning to register what is going on

Still he talks, he asks what am I thinking?

But I have no thoughts no words

There is nothing

My body has no words

I am in the hole

In the dark

Painful physical pain

Head pain constricted eyes

Seeing not believing

Not understanding

Feeling the perceived threat which doesn't match what is in front of me

Someone I trust is talking to me

He doesn't threaten me

I am in a safe environment

Where I feel safe

Where I trust this person

It is very confusing

Still he talks

I begin to take in what is going on

I feel a full body release of my muscles and tension

My big muscles, I have relaxed a degree

I am able to understand more and begin to utter words

After another minute I feel a second full body release of my tensed muscles

The physical threat has been released

I must process the intellectual side

He says rejection is a core issue for me

That any rejection destroys me and my reaction is total

This is my experience of rejection

Even with someone I know

Who poses no threat,

This is what I experience

What does it mean?

This is an extraordinary micro account of what happens when the defensive self is triggered in the therapy room by the actions of the caregiver. It shows that Jean could remain present to herself and to be aware of what was getting aroused in her, while also taking in information about the way the other person was responding to her. It was like she was in the process of coming into a new understanding of relationship. She was able to retain her own experience of the caregiver in front of her, even though what he was doing was resonating with a less benign past lodged in her internal environment and influencing her current responses.

Jean's fear system is immediately triggered by hearing the words 'We need to talk about you wanting to hold my hand'. She went into the freeze aspect of her system for self-defence. However, we can also see she is processing at a much deeper place. She felt she had done something wrong, which is her internal environment working in an unsupportive way. We go into this in more detail in Chapter Seven. She was reminded of previous experiences of being rejected by an old boyfriend, and by her parents at a more subconscious or preverbal level. In those incidents she would have supported herself in the past by saying, 'Never let them know they hurt you!', 'Turn and walk away!'. This time she stayed, and told me what it felt like. This took a long time and we returned to the theme of rejection over the next weeks and months, as stated in the previous chapter. This work took over a year to complete.

Jean was able to track her own bodily responses almost second by second. The first thing to notice is the amount of references to her body and bodily reactions:

'My physical reaction was the first responder'

'My head was bursting with all the tension'

'My body had no words'

As she experienced her own fearful state she was able to process how I was responding to her:

'Speaking in a low calm voice, his eyes were soft and matched his words'

As she processed this response from her caregiver she could experience a change in her defensive structure:

'I feel a full body release … My big muscles, I have relaxed a degree'

This leads to a remarkable transformation in Jean's dynamic organization, moving from frozen fear to curiosity:

'I must process the intellectual side'

'He says rejection is a core issue for me'

'This is my experience, what does it mean?'

The caregiver's reactions

How did O'Toole, as the caregiver, keep from becoming frightened or acting out of his own system for self-defence? O'Toole continues the narrative here in the first person.

I knew it was the right thing to do to address the issue of holding my hand and that I was not doing it to hurt or reject Jean. I knew she trusted me. I also felt I had created more space and freedom having addressed the issue as I had kept my chair in its usual position. I had to do enough at that moment to support Jean to remain in the room with me, as it would take a lot of work to process what had happened in this change in our relationship. I knew it was important to keep reminding Jean not to make the need wrong, and that she had done nothing wrong. I felt this was the crucial bit of information for me to get across, and also for me to support myself that I had not done anything wrong in spite of the strong transference from Jean.

What Jean was going though was paralleled with what I as the caregiver was experiencing. I initially thought all our work for six years was lost, but I was able to steady and recover myself. My natural response to fear is to withdraw into a very silent place within myself and to feel I have done something wrong; this is my defensive self. However, through my own training and involvement in this work I have been able to understand my own silence in a very deep and powerful way. As with all professional caregivers, the original organization of my internal structure continues to exist, but I have been able to create new pathways within myself that meant I had a lot more freedom to remain present to what was happening in my own internal environment, and between me and my client.

I was relieved to read in Jean's account that what I did was to keep talking to her in an empathic and regulating way, using my voice and my presence as instrument.

> 'He is leaning towards me
>
> Speaking in a low, calm voice.
>
> His eyes are soft and match his words.
>
> I heard him say "you have done nothing wrong"
>
> He didn't stop talking,
>
> He kept talking, still he talks …
>
> Someone I trust is talking to me'

I am using my voice, my tone, the melody of my voice matched with my facial expression and the expression in my eyes, I am leaning forward towards her, full body engagement to reach someone who has disappeared inside herself in terror. I am not gone into fear myself but am using my full emotional cognitive mental and physical facilities in this moment to reach someone I know very well but who is in trouble and needs the right response that is immediate, confident, coherent, and clearly full square on her side.

If I had gone into fear I may have stopped talking, or stopped trying to reach Jean. I would have put the onus on Jean to come out herself from a place of terror, which she would not have been able to do. All her resources at that time were focused on survival, and we know from our understanding of the fear system that the goal of the fear system is survival. Someone in the throes of their full fear system will not look for help but will try to survive as best they can on their own. What is required of the caregiver is to give an immediate, strong, and unambiguous response, not to go into fear themselves, and to help the person navigate their way from fear to careseeker, all within the system for self-defence.

Having this theoretical understanding allowed me to see Jean's behaviour of holding my hand as a form of careseeking. My job was to help Jean to explore how to verbalize her need that was not met at a preverbal level. This aspect of the self could only be accessed when her fear system was triggered to its highest peak by her caregiver, who she felt at that moment was rejecting her.

The keystone system for Jean's internal organization was her defensive self. It is her reliance on her system for self-defence, for her survival and protection, that dominated all her interactions, and as a result any threat to this system of defence would be guarded against at all cost. Regulating that fearful terrified state was key to allowing Jean to come into relationship with herself and with me in a new way through her careseeking self, separate from her defensive self and as a separate human being. Through the work with me as her caregiver, Jean's defensive closed system was able to be opened; allowing her core internal dynamic organization to be challenged and the Restorative Process (Heard, Lake & McCluskey, 2009/12) within all of the different systems within her attachment dynamic to take root.

LeDoux (1998) tells us that 'we should take defensive behaviours at face value, they represent the operation of brain systems that have been programmed by evolution to deal with danger in routine ways' (p. 128). He goes on to say that, 'In fact defence reactions should be thought of as constantly changing dynamic solutions to the problem of survival. They are not static structures created in ancestral species and maintained unchanged. They change as the world in which they operate changes' (LeDoux, 1998, p. 133). This is a very good description of the fear/danger aspect of the defensive self, or the second circuit of the vagus nerve (Porges) and how it operates.

One of the things that LeDoux's (1998, 2012) research also tells us is that the fear system is lightning fast and occurs at the level below conscious awareness. How we as humans, and non-humans, integrate these older systems designed for biological survival (second and third circuits of the vagus nerve) with the newer attachment/careseeking system, also designed for survival but survival with well-being, is what TABEIS (the theory of attachment-based exploratory interest sharing, developed by Dorothy Heard and Brian Lake) has managed to achieve. It provides a bridge between the field of biology and psychology and it is finding empirical support in the neuroscience revolution, which is the current wave in the field of psychotherapy.

Finally, LeDoux (1998) points out that 'fear can be lurking in the background of many kinds of emotions, that on the surface might seem to be the antithesis of fear'. I believe that when we experience or meet particular presentations of behaviour that are the antithesis of fear – be it compliance, lack of affect, or the absence of a verbal narrative – we need to be alert to the role of fear in such presentations. We will explore this in greater detail in Chapter Seven.

Jean described this piece of work as:

> by far the hardest and greatest learning experience for me. It exposed an issue so deep rooted that, when it was out and 'live', it took a great deal of caring and courage from myself and the therapist to navigate a way through it.

Chapter 6

One's internal environment

The keystone system as the source of the transference: an exploration of lack of personal narrative and the presentation of psychosomatic symptoms

In this chapter we explore the internal environment. This is the one aspect of the self that does not have a set goal in Bowlby's terms and therefore is not goal-corrected. In this book we put forward the view that the internal environment as an aspect of the self is dynamically changed and updated on the basis of whether the different goal-corrected systems which we explore reach, or fail to reach, their biological goal. When the person has the experience of being facilitated to reach the goal of a particular system (which has been aroused), through the help of an effective caregiver, their internal environment will be updatd based on that experience. When the person does not have this experience, the internal world is not updated, it retains in a particular organization. What is happening to the self when the internal environment is not being updated will be explored throughout the chapter, as will what needs to happen in order for the Restorative Process (Heard, Lake & McCluskey, 2009/12) to be kick-started onto a new developmental trajectory.

The history of psychoanalysis has in one way or another been an attempt to uncover the workings of the internal environment. As Symington puts it, 'Psychoanalysis is a method of investigating the unconscious mind and its particular focus is on the inner world' (Symington, 1986, p. 16). In this chapter we are looking at the internal environment and how it is connected to the other systems or aspects of the self in the context of the theoretical framework of Heard and Lake (1997) and the Restorative Process which they introduced in 2009. 'We consider that the place we have called the internal environment corresponds to the internal world that is referred to by analysts, although we also consider that the details of the internal world vary somewhat between different analytic schools (Heard, Lake & McCluskey, 2009/12, p. 45).

For us the concept of the internal environment provides us with the idea of an environment which can influence the self. We explore this aspect of the self in the context of our new understanding of transference and counter-transference, from an attachment perspective. This will shed light on the process of change, which occurs within the dynamic organization of the self.

Where this has not been one's experience of how other people have responded and related to you, it takes a long time for a different experience of interaction to be embedded inside of oneself. For the person to change their ideas and beliefs about how other people will respond to them they will require a new bodily based experience in order to update their experience of how they are being responded to, and how they view themselves within their own internal environment. This change can only come about experientially, and by the person seeking care and taking in a new type of interaction that allows them to experience subjectively what it is like to reach the goal of careseeking. We refer to this as 'rearranging the internal furniture'.

As we have said in Chapter One, we are extending the meaning of the term transference from its original meaning. The analysis of the transference was initially seen as an important and necessary part of freeing the person from the 'repetition compulsion' (Freud, 1914). Coltart states that, in his 1914 paper, Freud is concentrating on remembering, repeating, and working through in the transference. She is pointing out that, even in insightful patients, repressed emotions and early experiences incapable of coming straight into memory may appear as transference feelings and behaviours that then enable the analyst to make accurate translations and thus broaden the self-experience of the patient (Coltart, 1996, p. 66).

In our model of exploratory goal-corrected psychotherapy we focus on the interaction between therapist and client itself, and, based on McCluskey's (1999, 2005, 2009) work, show how the interaction itself needs to be goal-corrected in order to influence and update the internal environment of the person seeking help. This fundamentally changes the relationship between the two participants. It places the therapist in the role of an active, involved, and participating caregiver, rather than the neutral observing and interpreting analyst who is a blank screen for the transference of infantile projections, fantasies, and defences. In this way what we are looking at is how to apply the concept of goal-correction to change in the internal environment of the adult and child; as the child undergoes development, and the adult as they engage in exploratory psychotherapy.

Transference from a historical perspective didn't take account of biological goals of a person's sense of self in all these different dimensions. Psychoanalysis limited itself to focusing on a person's inner world based on their experience of others or, more importantly in the work of Freud, their fantasized experiences of others. It was Bowlby who made the fundamental point that what we incorporate into the self is our actual experience of relationships and the world around us (see the last interview with Bowlby, by Virginia Hunter, 2015). The analyst was, through their training, seen as immune to the influence of their own countertransference onto the patient.

The work of Daniel Stern (1985) is crucial to this emerging understanding. In the Introduction to the new edition of his 1995 book, 'The Interpersonal World of the Infant', he writes that:

The central idea that internal objects are constructed from repeated, relatively small interactive patterns, derived from the microanalytic perspective. Such internal objects are not people, nor are they parts or aspects of others. Rather, they are constructed from the patterned experience of self in interaction with another. What is inside (i.e., represented internally) comprises interactive experience ... This view of the internal object world was a departure from most of those prevailing at the time in dynamic psychotherapies.

(Stern, 2000, p. xv)

From this perspective our internal environment is made up of repeated interactive patterns which have their origins in our earliest interactions with attachment figures. Fairbairn (1952) called these dynamic relationships structures 'internal objects'; Bowlby (1979) called them internal working models; Heard and Lake (1997) called them 'internal models of the experience of relationships' in order to differentiate them from the fact that we create internal working models of all experience; and Stern (1985) called them 'experiences of relationships that are generalised' (McCluskey, 2005, p. 34).

It is Stern's work on attunement that is of most significance here, in terms of developing our understanding of the nature of these interactive patterns, and the work of McCluskey in building on Stern's work in relation to goal-corrected empathic attunement as the key factor in determining if a pattern of interaction between a caregiver and a careseeker was successful or not in the adult psychotherapy context. By 2000, Stern called these interactive patterns 'ways-of-being-with, de-emphasizing the process of formation in favour of describing the lived phenomenon in a more experience near and clinically useful way' (Stern, 2000, p. xv).

Stern goes on to explain that 'researchers working within the new perspective of an embodied mind, where the traditional sharp separation between body and mind is no longer maintained, have provided insights into the nature of a primary consciousness, that is usable in infancy' (Stern, 2000, p. xvii). This new sense of an embodied mind consists of several parts. 'The first is that all mental acts (perception, feeling, cognition, remembering) are accompanied by input from the body including internal sensations ... this input is what Damasio (1994, 2000) has called "background feelings", which are similar to the vitality affects introduced in the present (1985) book' (Stern, 2000, p. xvii). It is this connection with the body which is the foundation of his idea of 'affect attunement' which has proved to be most useful clinically, and is the bedrock of the advances made by the neuroscience researchers such as Siegel (1999), Schore (2003b, 2003c, 2012), Porges (2004, 2011) and Ogden, Minton and Pain (2006).

However, it is the work of Susan Vas Dias who explores the question 'Why the experience of affect is so central in human development...' (Vas Dias, 2000, p. 160) that has been the most useful clinically for us and the type of people who present for therapy, particularly long-term individual work. The work of Vas Dias builds on that of Stern (1985), Bowlby (1979) and Allen Schore (2003a) and combines these modern theories with her own training as a child psychoanalyst with Anna Freud, at the Anna Freud Centre, to provide what she describes as developmental help. Developmental help is defined as 'therapeutic help which is based on an understanding of the stresses and strains of infant and childhood emotional development and the problems which can arise at various times during that development' (Vas Dias, 2000, p. 167). In view of the developments there have been in our understanding of the internal environment, the internal world, and the emotional world, it is easy to forget the importance of this simple statement, that developmental help is based on 'an understanding of the stresses and strains of infant and childhood emotional development'. The basic premise of Vas Dias' thesis is that 'emotional experience is always accompanied by visceral arousal ... this means that our affective world is intricately intertwined with our physical being, the very foundation of the experience of ourselves' (Vas Dias, 2000, p. 160).

In O'Toole's work with several of the male clients that he sees he is aware that many of these men who came for help are unable to verbalize how they felt when they first entered therapy. He located the silence of these men as a communication from within the system for self-defence in the theoretical framework of Heard and Lake (O'Toole, 2015).

The experience of not having careseeking needs met in the first weeks and months of the infant's life, when they are primarily physical in nature, results in one's internal environment not been integrated between affect and cognition and symbolic representation. At the preverbal stage of developing, the infant is dependent on the mother to meet his or her physical needs and to label those needs in a way that the infant can recognize what these sensations mean when they experience them in their body. In the absence of this process of labelling of one's visceral experience at this early stage, there is a failure to know what one experiences in one's body as an adult or adolescent. When this happens the result is a failure to know oneself and to make oneself known to the other person. When this experience continues over time, stemming from the experience of not having one's early non-verbal careseeking signals responded to by a responsive and empathic caregiver, the result is the experience of not knowing how to verbalize one's emotional experience, which then becomes enacted in so many different forms of silence.

This aspect of silence within the system for self-defence shows itself in the interaction between the therapist and the client in many different guises. One such example is when the client is unable to bring material to work on in the session. If the therapist is not able to respond to the many non-verbal clues that are on display, despite the absence of a verbal narrative, the client will remain shut down and not be able to enter a therapeutic relationship with the therapist. This is where the work of Beebe and Lachmann's (2002, 2005, 2014) extensive research on a systems model of the interaction between infants and mother and its relevance for psychoanalysis has been most illuminating.

According to Beebe and Lachmann, 'empirical infant research describes processes that lie beyond the usual verbal exchange. Especially with "difficult-to-treat" patients, this attention to the interactive process itself, analogous to frame-by-frame analysis, makes a critical contribution to therapeutic leverage' (Beebe & Lachmann, 2002, p. 23).

Recognizing in this presentation a re-enactment of an early attachment dynamic, where the client as the infant or child was not adequately responded to by their attachment figure, the therapist needs to be responsive to the physical non-verbal aspects of the client's presentation, just like the mother had to be responsive to the physical needs of the infant at the beginning of their life when in a state of complete physical dependence. The mother needs to be responsive to the wet nappies, the child's temperature, the colour of the skin, whether the baby feeds or not, if the baby has had enough sleep or whether he or she needs a nap. The therapist has to be alert to the physical presentation of the client; are they warm or cold, have they enough clothes, are they coughing, what physical ailments are they suffering from? (See the account of Martin later in this chapter, who presents with physical symptoms of a very tight gut and a piercing pain in his forehead. There is no narrative except the presentation of physical symptoms.) How is the person responding verbally or non-verbally, are they spontaneous, slow to respond, are they able to explore how they feel about something, or does the person just respond to whatever is asked of them and wait for the next question? In our work we explicitly check if the person is able or willing to take a step by letting us, the caregiver, help them. Until we have their cooperation no exploration will be possible. This work seeks to explore the permeability or un-permeability at the boundary between the self and the other. We encourage the client to check if they are curious about what is happening in the interaction, while being mindful of the dangers of the client submitting to the authority of the therapist, which is antithetical to the exploratory process.

The client who is unable to verbalize their emotions directly will expect the therapist to know intuitively without having to tell them or enter into a relationship with the other person. They do not expect to be responded to even though they are hoping that, just by turning up, they will find some relief. 'Embedded in the psychoanalytic relationship is the patient's hope to be emotionally known and understood (Bromberg, 1998) ... This unique mix of promise on the one hand and the perceived threat triggered by it on the other, seems to rekindle and reproduce the neutrally encoded memory networks' (Ginot, 2007, p. 324). Similarly, 'the therapeutic relationship activates the dreaded, dissociated maladaptive emotional schema that brought the patient into treatment in the first place. At the same time, these very same patterns are the ones that he simultaneously wants to examine and to avoid' (Bucci, 2005, p. 861, in Ginot, 2007, pp. 324–325).

However, as Beatrice Beebe observes, 'the co-construction of the inter-subjective field is currently of great interest to psychoanalysis, detailed clinical material illustrating the nonverbal and implicit dimension of this process remains rare' (Beebe et al., 2005, p. 89). Beebe further states that, as Lyons-Ruth (1999) notes, 'much remains to be learned about how implicit modes of intimate relating are transformed and about the analyst specific collaborative participation in this process, as a new kind of relational partner' (p. 612).

Beebe (2005) goes on to describe in great detail aspects of verbal as well as non-verbal implicit processes in the ten-year treatment of a client she refers to as Delores, and Beebe's own particular collaborative participation. While the account of this treatment needs to be read in its own right, I am struck by one of the concluding comments from Beebe that:

> One of the most essential aspects of what was reparative in this treatment was Delores's sense that she could affect me and that I could affect her. She could sense and see and see again in the video how her agony impacted on me, shifted my face and voice, created tenderness in me and comforting.
>
> (Beebe, 2005, p. 137)

In analysing the work using a dyadic systems point of view, Beebe suggests that:

> This basic concept of the mutual regulation model that each partner affects the other is broader than the concept of matching. It indicates that each partner senses in herself an ongoing receptivity (or lack of receptivity) to the other, in adjusting, tracking and being 'influenced' as well as an ongoing impact (or failure of impact) on the other. This is the bedrock of the entire treatment, the foundation of all human communication. Matching is a very specific form of this more general process of bidirectional interactive regulation.
>
> (Beebe, 2005, p. 137)

McCluskey picks up this same process in the adult domain:

> The caregiver by his voice tone (which is serious and entirely focused), his choice of words, the fact that he goes straight for the affect that the careseeker is experiencing, and takes a risk on naming it as well as showing through the expression on his face that he has been affected himself by what the careseeker has said, provides affect containment and regulation as well as an empathic connection.
>
> (McCluskey, 2005, p. 231)

Case study

Martin is a young man in his early thirties who came to O'Toole for therapy for a number of severe physical symptoms he is suffering from. These symptoms consist of a severe pain and tightness in his gut, a piercing pain in his forehead, and very low energy levels. This linking of the psyche and soma was very striking for me in how Martin presented. I found the work of Susan Vas Dias really helpful in working with this case, and how this lack of integration between Martin's physical and mental well-being was completely separate in his world view.

Presentation

The first thing that I noticed about my dealings with this man was that when he contacted me I recommended he get in touch with a colleague of mine as I was not in a position to take him on as a client at the time. I did not think any more about him until two weeks later, when Martin contacted me to inform me that the person I had recommended he see for therapy was not in a position to see him. I immediately felt something about the need to respond to this man's request to be seen, and there was something about the start of this connection that was significant. There was something about him being forgotten and not being noticed or responded to from the beginning. He had to work hard to be seen and heard.

I arranged to see Martin and he presented as a very small, slightly built man in his mid-thirties. I was immediately able to see how he could have been forgotten and left behind. He described in detail a recurring pain in his gut, which he said 'is always there'. He also described a piercing pain in his forehead and a lack of energy. He said he had tried various physical treatments, which had had no effect, and that he wanted to see if psychological treatment could be of any help to him.

Martin presented his physical symptoms with very little affect and with very little other narrative. His whole being appeared preoccupied by his physical symptoms, especially his low energy levels which affected every aspect of his life, his ability to work, and his interactions with colleagues and friends.

My countertransference to Martin was of distress, but also some level of interest and challenge. What had happened to this man's energy, his vitality, his ability to lead a normal life? In the model we are presenting here, a question to ask ourselves is 'what system is being aroused in you in response to this man?' In relation to Martin it was my exploratory caregiving system that was aroused. This is evident in my willingness to take Martin on as a client. Martin explained how his symptoms were affecting his sense of taste, his sense of smell, and he did not know when he felt hungry or not or whether he was tired or not. His whole world was dominated by these physical symptoms, which appeared to have no obvious physical cause.

Martin had had many consultations with doctors and consultants without finding any insight or reason for his physical symptoms. These experiences of failed careseeking could only reinforce Martin's unsupportive internal environment that nobody could help him. In one of his most recent consultations with me, Martin informed me that when he was six weeks old he was hospitalized for a heart operation; this came when I shared my own bodily based sense that what Martin was describing to me at the time in relation to his body symptoms felt 'very young'. This links with recent evidence, such as that of Luyten and De Meulemeester (2017) who suggest that 'attachment theory has played a vital role in furthering our understanding of patients with persistent somatic complaints.… The origins of these complaints are often insufficiently understood' (Luyten & De Meulemeester, 2017, pp. 206–207). These authors go on to say that 'current evidence-based treatments often do not adequately take into account existing knowledge concerning interpersonal and attachment issues in the treatment of these disorders' (p. 207).

Martin presented like this for a number of sessions, beginning each session with the same list of symptoms with no variation in tone, in affect or delivery. It was mesmerizing to listen to; it was also numbing in its effect, meaning that due to the absence of affect this man was experienced by me as boring and wooden. Along with his lack of variation in tone, temperament, and delivery, his facial muscles gave no indication of what he was experiencing. This is a good example of what Porges (2004) talks about; i.e., when the facial muscles are not conveying emotion and the social engagement system is not operating. In Porges' terms, the person has gone to the second stage of defence of fight and flight, or the third stage of immobilization. Porges makes the point that when the person is recruiting the vagus nerve in this way, it can affect the proper functioning of the organs in the body. In our words, the careseeking system is being infiltrated by the system for self-defence as shown in the lack of expression on the face or in the voice.

The first clue I got into this man's difficulties was when I picked up on the speed and intensity in how he answered any question, without taking a second to consider what was being asked or to reflect before answering. As he doesn't leave any pause for reflection, Martin is unable to let anything into his system. He was blocking any engagement, although he had no sense of doing so at any level of his being. His intensity appeared to come from his desire to be rid of his symptoms, and he thought by telling me what his symptoms were I would be able to help him get rid of them. He had no other thought. There was no evidence of any curiosity as to what these symptoms might mean or what they were trying to convey.

After five sessions of regular attendance I received a call from Martin to ask if he could cancel his appointment and if I could see him during the week. I was surprised by the phone call and checked if everything was okay. I was aware no information was offered in regard to a reason for needing to cancel the appointment. I rearranged his appointment for two days later. When he arrived he made no mention of the cancelled appointment. He immediately went into a description of his symptoms, which had not changed. I was surprised by the fact that he did not mention anything about having to cancel his appointment. He acknowledged that I had enquired when we were speaking on the phone if there was anything wrong as to why he was unable to attend. He said he was aware of not giving me any information at the time on the phone; 'I suppose I'm cagey' he said. I smiled.

Martin informed me that his mother had arrived at his flat and he did not want to tell her he was going for counselling, so he decided to cancel his appointment with me and to request a different appointment that week. This gave me further insight into this man's relationship with both himself and his primary attachment figure. He also spoke about often experiencing many feelings of guilt that he had done something wrong, and how he deals with such feelings by pushing them down and not giving away any information.

He also told me he expects to be criticized. This helped me to better understand this man's manner of engaging. It is as if he is on the stand in a court facing the prosecution and having to account for what he had done.

I have continued to work with Martin over the past number of months. His attendance is excellent and he enjoys coming to the sessions with me. He has a positive transference to me and says he trusts me, even though he can see how at times he still struggles to open up to me about how he feels. At moments of heightened affect his body stiffens considerably. At other times his body begins to shake and tremble. This movement can start off in his arm relatively slowly, but it can escalate to quite a rapid pace. During this time I encourage Martin to remain in eye contact with me and to keep his feet on the ground.

I have worked primarily to help him centre in the chair, to breathe into his body, and into the physical block which he describes as 'like a rock in his gut'. Helping Martin to breathe and to slow down is allowing him to hear something of the anguish in his body, even though he has no words for this pain. He is beginning to think about the possibility that there may be a connection between his physical self and his emotional or internal world. Listening to the sound of his breathing is like listening to the high-pitched screams of a young child who has been forgotten. I relate this back to him in a way that he can acknowledge.

Martin feels his energy levels have improved since attending therapy with me, and his bowels and gut have relaxed over the past few weeks. Learning to attune to the absence of a verbal narrative and the presentation of physical symptoms has underlined for me the significance of Vas Dias' statement that 'the difficulties with which a person is struggling often give an indication at which developmental level their problems arose. Once this becomes clear, appropriate developmental help can be provided' (Vas Dias, 2000, p. 164).

This means that, by being aware of the fact that most of Martin's somatic symptoms are in his gut and stomach, this is very early trauma work (recall his early separation when six weeks old). It needs to be done slowly and carefully in order for Martin to begin to translate his symptoms into words. In order to do this he will need to feel safe in the therapeutic space with me. These symptoms have their origin in the early caregiving of this man as a very young child, a very hostile environment at home, and perhaps the distress of his primary caregiver from a very young age at a preverbal level. This is something we know from the research; that very small babies attune to the state of the other and this can result in confusion as to what emotions, sensations, and thoughts belong to oneself or the other person that one is attuning to.

Renn (2012) states that 'Research indicates that developmental trauma is typically embedded in the child's family situation and so is not merely a single event phenomenon but cumulative (Khan, 1979, McDougall, 1985, 1989, Rutter, 1981, 1997, Schore, 1994, Wilkinson, 2010). As a result of such severe misattunement, the infant is left for long periods in an intensely disorganized psychobiological state that is beyond his or her coping strategies' (Renn, 2012, p. 25).

It was Khan (1974) who introduced the concept of cumulative trauma, which he says 'has its beginnings in the period of development when the infant needs and uses the mother as his protective shield ... Where these failures of the mother in her role as protective shield are significantly frequent and lead to impingements on the infant's psych-soma, impingements which he has no means of eliminating, they set up a process of interplay with the mother which is distinct from her adaptation to the infant's needs' (p. 53). Elsewhere Khan suggests, 'One treacherous aspect of cumulative trauma is that it operates and builds up silently throughout childhood right up to adolescence' (p. 56).

A more modern take on this process of cumulative trauma would more likely talk about:

> the internalisation of such interactive patterns and how they may interfere with the developing child's optimal regulation of arousal and thus comprise his or her capacity to stay attentive and to process socio-emotional information and regulate bodily states, particularly when under heightened emotional stress.
>
> (Renn, 2012, p. 25)

The emphasis on the dysregulation of bodily functions such as the gut and bowels is particularly pertinent in the case of Martin.

In a recent session Martin was able to articulate much more clearly the strong connection between the stress he feels in the presence of his father and the impact on his body. 'My bowel just shut down,' he said. He was able to remain present in his body while sitting at the kitchen table as his father was also present in the room. He noticed how his body and his bowels in particular shut down immediately after this visit and how his energy was very chaotic, meaning he could not settle for a number of hours after he went home and had to take the following day off work. This was in contrast to the previous session, which was his first with me following the Christmas break, during which he shared a lot. However, instead of feeling drained, as he had previously felt following our sessions, Martin said he felt energized and was able to go to work the following day, which was a change for him. The change in vitality is the kind of evidence that we use within the model of exploratory goal-corrected psychotherapy of how self is facilitated to move from self-defence to exploration in the context of the interaction with an exploratory caregiver.

In the case of Martin he is aware of not wanting to burden his mother with his own anxieties and difficulties in dealing with his feelings towards his father, as she has enough on her plate. This is something we have not been able to explore yet. However, this may well signal an overreliance on a defensive caregiving role in order to cope with the pain and distress that he has been living with for quite some time.

He is also beginning, as he sits in the sessions with me, to connect his need to respond as if he were facing the prosecution on the stand in a court room when he hears his father's voice and sees his face in front of him. Martin is confused as he always thought none of this affected him, because he told himself that he would rise above it and not be affected by how his father treated him.

This presentation clearly demonstrates the link between early trauma and bodily symptoms, and the absence of a verbal narrative for one's emotional world. His early signals for care and protection were missed and not responded to. His defensive strategy of defensive caregiving to his mother became an early coping mechanism which has left it difficult for him to seek care in a straightforward manner. Martin describes his body as heavy and devoid of energy, and his mind as constantly racing, unable to pause long enough to consider what course of action to take. Epstein notes that:

> Up until the mid-eighties the world of medicine perceived the brain and the body to have two separate and unconnected immune systems. Therefore, those who suggested a link between the psycho and the soma were considered wishful thinkers or new age healers who were experimenting with alternative medicine.
>
> (Epstein, 2017, p. 258)

However, when referring to her own practice she suggests that 'almost every person who has come to see me has expressed some form of mental anguish as well as some kind of bodily complaint such as: migraines, back pains, poor bowel movements, frequent colds, aching bones, skin irritations, chronic fatigue, thyroid problems and many other symptoms. To begin with, these physiological symptoms tend to invade the therapeutic space, in particular with clients who seem to display avoidant attachment styles of relating, as individuals with avoidant attachment styles tend to down play or internalise their emotions, and express them somatically' (Epstein, 2017, p. 260).

I notice myself helping Martin regulate how he presents from the moment he comes into the room. I encourage him to centre before he immediately goes into an account of his symptoms. I encourage him to check inside himself before he responds. I ask him to notice how he is breathing and to notice when he forgets to breathe. I attune to his physical tension and ask him to notice when his voice rises in pitch, as he tries to put an explanation on what he feels rather than just telling me what he is experiencing. Countering all these defensive reactions, helping Martin to slow down and regulate his intake and output of breath, is helping him to experience how his level of trust in me is growing. This work of affect attunement, affect identification, affect regulation, and goal-corrected empathic attunement is helping Martin to know when his fear system gets triggered and beginning to help him verbalize his experience.

It is important that I remain centred in my own body and not get frightened by Martin's many and rapid body movements, which can happen very quickly in the session. I respond in a calm voice, telling him to breathe and to look at me, and to tell me what is happening. I try to help him make sense of what is happening by tracking what he recalls happening just before his legs or arms start to shake.

This is the same detailed work that McCluskey does in her work with individuals in her exploratory groups, the difference being that, in working with the individual and the group at the same time, this is enabling the members of the group to tune into what is happening in their own bodies as they are listening and attuning to the work of the individual. In this way she is able to use the information that is transferred from one person to another through the way that they attune to what is happening in the body of the other. This can be exceedingly effective when done in a group context.

I am helping Martin to verbalize his emotions, rather than having to enact his feelings and regress to a point of being out of contact with me in the here and now of the therapeutic situation.

Discussion

In this work with Martin I was very aware of the absence of any verbal narrative about Martin's internal environment or his emotional world. This part of his life appeared to be switched off, perhaps like I was switched off to him when he first made contact with me for an initial appointment. His facial expression was often blank, and the first clue I got into this man's internal environment was the intensity and speed with which he responded to any question I would put to him. As I became aware of the impact in me of being with Martin, and the rapid replies that seemed to be his only mode of responding, I was able to feed back this information to him in an effort to help him notice how he was responding. I asked him to be aware of the impact of my questions on him, and how his response was not telling me anything I wanted to know, but were similar to a quick return of my serve in a tennis match, designed to nullify any further inquiries.

Once I became aware of this intensity and pace of the return I became more curious and it led to further inquiries. There are many more rallies happening now in our interactions.

The central question in relation to this case study is how do I as the therapist (caregiver) help Martin begin to feel that it is safe enough to verbalize his experience when he is with me so he does not feel so alone in his emotional world? Up to now, Martin's emotional world could only be communicated through the presentation of debilitating physical symptoms, which he has to try to manage on his own. By slowing down the process of asking the questions and asking Martin to allow some time before he answers, I am purposefully mis-attuning to his pace and intensity and not acting out the transference with his father; altering the contingency that he must respond immediately before something terrible happens to him. By intervening in the gap between the time I ask a question and when Martin responds, I am trying to upset the contingency that has formed in his mind from a very young age that something terrible will happen if he does not answer immediately. His only consideration is to answer quickly in an effort to ward off any further questions. Martin has made the connection between how he responds with me and how frightening and upsetting it has been for him when faced with his father's menacing series of questions.

In short, my work with Martin shows how the interactions between us has changed both participants. For my part I now have a much warmer response to Martin and am more open and curious about his internal environment, his emotional world which was completely absent when he first presented. I no longer find him boring or wooden, but am intrigued by what his hidden world could look and sound like if he is able to continue to verbalize his emotional experience. I can feel his affect of pain, sadness, loneliness, and anger at what he has had to suffer, and I continue to try to attune and give words to what his body is telling me in how he responds both verbally and non-verbally. Writing this case study shows the level of interest I now have for him, and I sense that he senses how I am interested in him as a fellow human being.

Conclusion

In this chapter we looked at how the internal environment is the one aspect of the self that is not goal-corrected. Instead it is an aspect of the self which is constantly updated or not updated, on the basis of whether the different goal-corrected behavioural systems identified by Heard and Lake reach or fail to reach their goal.

We explored how the importance of being able to experience affect is so vital to our perceptions of ourselves as unique individuals. This is something that Vas Dias has written extensively about. In her work she showed how our visceral experience of affect, felt through our bodies, forms the building blocks of how we experience ourselves and how we are responded to through the process of affect attunement.

We used the example of Martin to show how his only available means of communicating his distress was through bodily-based symptoms. This was a re-enactment of how his distress was not attuned to and regulated when he was an infant. His lack of a verbal narrative to communicate his internal world was a key factor in helping O'Toole identify the source of the distress in this type of presentation.

In the next chapter we look at regulating virulence in transference and countertransference in a group context, from an attachment perspective.

Chapter 7

Early misattunements re-enacted in a group context

Regulating virulence in the transference and countertransference from an attachment perspective

McCluskey (2001) developed a theory of interaction in adult life when the dynamics of careseeking and caregiving are elicited. She discovered that when careseeking was aroused in one person and caregiving was aroused in the other, the patterns of interaction that then ensued between them could take the form of at least twenty-five different arrangements, nine of which appeared with regularity and could be studied. Out of these nine patterns, only two were experienced subjectively and objectively as effective in regulating affect. In this situation the person who was careseeking felt met and ready to explore, and the person who was giving care felt relieved and ready for the next step.

What these gentle words can hide is that the emotions aroused in both parties when there is careseeking and caregiving can range from mild through moderate to severe in intensity. Only two of the patterns of interaction that develop during this engagement lead to relief and subsequent interest in exploration (McCluskey, 2005, pp. 189–238). This means that sometimes the outcomes of the interactions between careseekers and caregivers can be highly emotive, dysregulated, and potentially harming. We felt it was important that we addressed this scenario in the book. If hatred is to arise in the transference or countertransference, we can assume that its primal roots are in infancy and that the virulence of the feelings in the here and now will have been triggered by some 'lookalike' in the communication – verbal or non-verbal – between the two parties. How this is worked with by the caregiver will be different if it occurs in one-to-one therapy from how it will be worked with in group. This chapter mainly deals with what options are available to a group therapist when this dynamic arises in a group context.

We approach this subject from the perspective on attachment that we are offering in this book and the model of practice we describe as exploratory goal-corrected psychotherapy.

Fairbairn stated in his 'Synopsis of an Object Relations Theory of the Personality' (in Grotstein & Rinsley, 1994, pp. 34–36) 'there is no death instinct; aggression is a reaction to frustration or deprivation'. We would agree that when a person has been rejected, humiliated, dysregulated, and on the receiving end of many other forms of disrespectful and abusive behaviour, that the anger they experience towards the person relating to them in this way will be intense, sometimes intense enough to warrant the term hatred. Fairbairn postulated the existence of a dynamic structure within the self that enabled the person to deal with frustrating and sometimes horrific experiences of another person. In this dynamic structure, aspects of the self remained attached to the original person, who became idealized. In addition, an aspect of the self became attached to the frustrating or bad aspects of the other person, and a further aspect became attached to the exciting aspects of the other. Fairbairn considered that another aspect of the self was involved in repressing the origins of this dynamic scenario from consciousness.

Therapists and those in the caring professions can trigger a negative transference of the sort we are referring to here. Caregivers are particularly vulnerable as they are almost inviting the transference by the very nature of their role. In cases of extreme virulence directed towards the professional caregiver it is wise to consider, before engaging in an open and exploratory way, whether the person who is directing their anger towards you is open to reflection and is curious about the intensity of their emotion. If one's judgment is that the person is so in the grip of their hatred, it may be wisest to draw on one's own supportive system for self-defence and be firm and clear with the other about the nature of what can and cannot be done in this context. The caregiver should be aware that in some cases the person in the grip of hatred against them may want to harm them, physically, professionally or psychologically. How to handle this dynamic in the caregiving/careseeking relationship is an important issue. It is one that caregivers should be prepared for and be willing, when necessary, to engage legal and professional help.

Being the subject or object of virulent hatred can be a very disorganizing, dysregulating, and frightening experience. Holding firm as the caregiver about what can and cannot be explored at this time might not be as easy as it sounds. As a professional caregiver, one is aware that a careseeker's early history of caregiving is very likely to be present in the here and now and could be a template through which the current situation is being perceived by them. This should offer some forewarning of the way oneself may be perceived if minor or major misattunements occur within the therapeutic frame.

As this is a major and powerful phenomenon, when it is triggered in the person-to-person interaction required of this model of work it is important that the professional caregiver can access care for themselves in the form of discussion, education, and support. As with most other phenomena of an emotional nature that is occurring in a group or individual setting, as the facilitator, one attunes to the state the other is in. Therefore, if the other is attacking, we know their system for self-defence or their defensive self is likely to be aroused. We know that in the role of facilitator or professional caregiver we are likely to attune to this aspect of the other and so it is highly likely our own system for self-defence will activate as well. We now have the possibility that two people are communicating to one another from their defensive selves. In this state both are likely to miss crucial information that is present to them from each other and both are vulnerable to acting out in ways that could be potentially dangerous and harmful.

If this happens in a group situation it is important as the caregiver to centre and slow down, slow everything right down. What is happening at that moment is that one member of the group is extremely angry with the facilitator and, as said earlier, this can be potentially dysregulating for the facilitator and the group. The nature and force of the dysregulation will depend on many factors. The facilitator may not be dysregulated at all, they may be temporarily taken aback and slightly disorganized, they may be very disorganized, depending on the virulence of the transferential phenomena and their own attachment history and training in attachment dynamics. Whatever the effect on the facilitator, he or she at that moment needs to be able to access that aspect of themselves that can look after themselves well. This will be located in their defensive selves.

When the facilitator is the target of a virulent attack from a member of a group this is going to impact the rest of the group membership. It is likely to trigger 'lookalikes' in the internal environment of all those present. In turn this will trigger the arousal of different aspects of the self within those present. So, for some members it will be the fear aspect of their defensive selves which will be aroused, making them want to flee, join in the fight or become immobilized. Others will have their careseeking selves aroused, but the designated caregiver that is present is under attack. For others it may be that their caregiving selves are aroused, directed towards the attacker or the facilitator. For others it may be the hate aspect of their self-defence system, conscious or unconscious, fuelling sadistic or masochistic impulses. For others it may be their observer selves, a state of freedom within the self that is available, curious, and exploratory.

At the moment of attack from the member, the facilitator clearly needs, as said earlier, to slow down the process of interaction completely and validate, regulate, and articulate all that is going on. It is important to acknowledge the range of responses likely to be present in the room and to normalize them. How does the caregiver remain available and exploratory in this context, while being mindful of their own well-being?

Let us pause a moment to consider how anger in the group may be explored when the anger is from one member to another member. In this context, using this model, it is important that the facilitator steps in and suggests that the member direct their anger to the facilitator as a stand-in for the target member. That is the first intervention. This signals to the object of attack that they will not have to deal with the full force of the attack and that the facilitator is there to take care of both parties. It suggests to the person with the impulse to attack that there is a safe forum for them to have their full emotion and to explore the information contained therein. The facilitator also has to be mindful of the possible impact of this scenario on the rest of the group. We call this working with foreground and background.

The facilitator needs to take time to regulate the arousal of emotion in the group as a whole, encouraging all those present to centre (thus attempting to counter the impulse to respond to 'lookalikes' from the past) and to reduce tension in their bodies as they attune to the emotional dynamics of the room. Again, the facilitator normalizes this attunement process and indicates that the more the group can allow their tension levels to relax, and just to stay loosely centred and explorative, the less tension is carried by the two protagonists. All this active regulating and educative work in the group by the facilitator may allow the transferential element in the anger to be revealed and worked with in a safe environment. The process that enables this to happen is that the facilitator centres the whole group, reminds them that their own internal environment will be triggered in the way just mentioned, and that what is most important in this moment is for everyone to allow the facilitator to work, to take themselves off the hook of providing caregiving, and to work at lowering the tension in their bodies so that the person with the anger is not attuning to tension in the group. In this environment, exploration of the triggering issue can be explored.

When the facilitator is the target of the hatred, what does the facilitator do?

It is important that the facilitator is in touch with resources in their own system for self-defence and has access to a supportive internal environment. If they have a co-facilitator then they may need to announce to the group that they have their own caregiver in the room so the group does not have to become caregivers to the facilitator. This will relieve those in the room who have become frightened for the well-being of the facilitator, which may well be a transfer of concern they bring from childhood dramas. If there is no co-facilitator it is important that the facilitator has clear and uncluttered knowledge within themselves of who they have available in their real life outside the group who they can go to for exploratory care and with whom they can discuss this afterwards.

From the position of knowing one is not alone and that one is in the company of benign exploratory supports, one has (as the facilitator) the best chance of engaging the attacking member in a discussion about whether they are able and curious to take a next step. If the person remains in a closed system state and is not permeable to receiving any information from the facilitator verbally or non-verbally, and is intent on continuing to express their hatred, the best that might be achieved is for the facilitator from a centred stance to: (a) acknowledge the level of hatred that is directed towards them; (b) to be totally firm that everyone in the room stay in their seats to ensure that there is no acting out (the facilitator may need to make the distinction between feeling something and acting it out); (c) that the expression of hatred in itself is important, there is information in it if one is curious; and (d) there can be no developmental work achieved at this moment.

This is not a recipe for what to do, and this type of scenario will play out in different ways, but the principle being outlined here is that the caregiver requires to be in the presence of a caregiver themselves, whether internally or externally, so that they are able to respond in a firm, compassionate, and benign way to everybody present in the room.

As we have said, this eruption of virulence may have taken members of the group by surprise and will have triggered past experiences and 'lookalikes' or feared future experiences. Nobody in the room will be unaffected. The different experience for those present, and hopefully a reparative one, is how this dyad deals with the expression of hatred at that moment, knowing that the work is not finished, may never be resolved, but that there is a context where one can return to the scenario at another moment in time when the curiosity of all may be engaged in exploring the information about the self contained within. But, to be clear, at the moment of impasse it may well be necessary for the facilitator to take the lead, close the session with the above comment, and remind all present to access their caregivers, who they will have identified before starting the group as being available to them during the period of attendance in the group.

This is not easy work, it is highly skilled, and the caregiver may fail to manage the process in a way that provides an educative and restorative experience for everyone. These failures stay with the facilitator and are the price of engaging in explorative work with relational dynamics that have their roots in verbal and preverbal experiences for everyone concerned. This work is not driven by manual and formula for how to respond to others. It is a delicate process of growing in maturity and ability on the part of the designated caregiver.

John Bowlby (1979, p. 154) states, 'Clearly to do the work well requires of the therapist not only a good grasp of principles but also a capacity for empathy and for tolerating intense emotions. Those with a strongly organized tendency towards compulsive self-reliance are ill-suited to undertake it and are well advised not to'.

In all the above, the reader will have gleaned that the important principle governing attachment-based exploratory work is that the caregiver has available to them an exploratory caregiver that supports and educates them. This is not solo performance. This emphasizes the need for professional caregivers to be in a caregiving relationship themselves. This work can be turbulent. We are working with turbulent forces in ourselves and others. We pick up on this theme again in the next chapter.

Fairbairn's view was that when the person internalized what he called the 'bad object' that 'Internalization of the object is not just a product of a phantasy of incorporating the object orally, but is a distinct psychological process. Two aspects of the internalized object, viz. its exciting and frustrating aspects, are split off from the main core of the object and repressed by the ego...' (Grotstein & Rinsley, 1994, pp. 34–35). The main core of the internalized object, which is not repressed, is described as the ideal object or ego-ideal.

How might one prepare for work with the negative transference as a group facilitator?

One thing one might do is to explore one's own feelings towards a person who attacks you. Are we aware of the nature of our anger toward others when they criticize or attack us? How do our separate emotions of fear and anger interact in such circumstances? Are we just aware of fear? Are we only aware of anger or rage? Are we unaware of what we feel? Are we frozen? Are we immobilized? An important part of any training in attachment-based work must involve helping to prepare would-be caregivers for the response to mis-attunements and to become familiar with their own defensive selves and the nature and workings of their defensive system. The most important aspect in training for this work is enabling the person to grow sufficiently to be able to discriminate and access good care for themselves and to act on this when they experience a threat to the self. It is very important that we develop the capacity to seek care for ourselves, care that is supportive and educative.

Compulsive self-reliance is clearly driven by the fear system. McCluskey's research using her database of professional caregivers showed that a high proportion of caregivers from all the different professions tend to rely on their fear system for survival and are loath to seek care (McCluskey & Gunn, 2015). We need therefore to take seriously the needs of people who enter caregiving professions and put in place adequate supports for them. We explore the nature of this phenomenon in the next chapter.

Chapter 8

When one's caregiving self is the keystone system

An exploration of data from McCluskey's work with over 800 professional caregivers who explored the dynamics of attachment in their own lives

This chapter shifts the focus from the consulting rooms of professional caregivers, working with those who have sought their help, to the dynamics of attachment in the caregivers themselves. Since the early 2000s McCluskey has been facilitating experiential courses for professional caregivers where the focus has been on exploring the dynamics of attachment in adult life. Initially her interest was in trying to understand the theory developed by Heard and Lake, which had extended Bowlby's two goal-corrected systems – careseeking and caregiving – to include sexuality, interest sharing, and personal self-defence. They had also added a further two systems that a person used when distressed and could not reach another person who could help. These systems were the internal environment (the images and templates people had retained of how others had helped them in the past when they were alarmed and frightened), and their personally created external environment, which is what they put together in the way of a supportive and home base.

The origin of McCluskey's interest in the work of Heard and Lake

McCluskey had been in a research group at the University of York for many years with Dorothy Heard and Brian Lake. Their book, 'The Challenge of Attachment for Caregiving', was published in 1997. Several seminars of the research group were devoted to trying to understand what these systems were about and how they worked. In the meantime, around 1994/95, McCluskey had started her own research into affect attunement in adult psychotherapy, inspired by Daniel Stern's work with infants. It was through this work and her research into the nature of the interaction between adult therapists and their clients that she began to see that the offer to treat itself aroused the dynamics of attachment in both the 'caregiver' and the 'careseeker' and that, whatever happened next, the caregiver had to regulate the emotional response of the careseeker to seeking help before the careseeker was in any position at all to explore what had brought them into therapy. She identified the process by which therapists managed to do this as goal-corrected empathic attunement (GCEA), the goal being to regulate the fear of the client (their defensive selves) which was activated and trumping their careseeking selves. It was the behaviours of the fear system that the therapist was faced with – fight, flight, fight and flight, freeze, collapse/shutdown. And, of courses, these same behaviours could be triggered in the therapist if their fear system got aroused and trumped their capacity for exploratory caregiving. So, she began to focus on the pattern of interaction between therapist and client as the key focus for intervention.

It was at this point (when she observed the dynamics of attachment at play in the therapeutic space) that she really connected with the work of Heard and Lake, whose work, as said, she was familiar with but did not fully understand.

At the same time, she was exploring insights from her work with Yvonne Agazarian in the US, with whom she had been collaborating since the early 1990s. Initially she had seen a connection between the way Agazarian was promoting sub-groups within the group as a whole and Fairbairn's endopsychic structure of the personality, and was riveted by the group techniques that Agazarian and her colleagues were developing for working with aspects of the self. McCluskey trained with Agazarian for more than ten years and became the first person in Europe to be licensed in Systems Centered Theory and Practice (SCT). By then she was moving away from object relations theory and more deeply into attachment theory as a framework for understanding human behaviour, and started bringing that emphasis to her work within the Institute for Systems Centered Theory and Practice.

It took a while for McCluskey to grasp that, while systems-centred work looked 'as if' it was working within an analytic framework based on Fairbairnian object relations, it seemed to have a different framework for understanding developmental process during the earliest relationship, and also that the work of Heard, Lake, and herself was significantly different in essential elements (McCluskey, 2002, 2008). She is aware from conversations with Agazarian just before her death in 2017 that SCT is now exploring the person system, and notes that the person is conceptualized as a system within which there are sub-systems expressed interpersonally as role relationships. This remains a difference from McCluskey's attachment-based model. The term 'system' is defined differently within the two models and the need for a careseeker to have an exploratory caregiver available to them is essential in attachment-based work.

Setting out to investigate the work of Heard and Lake with professional caregivers

It was with this background that McCluskey started an investigation into the theoretical model that Heard and Lake were developing for understanding the dynamics of attachment in adult life.

McCluskey therefore started her investigation with:

1   An interest in Heard and Lake's seven systems and how they worked.
2   Training in group facilitation: originally with Dr J.D. Sutherland in Edinburgh at the Scottish Institute of Human Relations; then as staff on Tavistock Group Relations Courses under the aegis of Harold Bridger; and finally a training with Dr Yvonne Agazarian.
3   Her own research into affect attunement in adult psychotherapy, which enabled her to understand that if the group facilitator is not responsive to group members when they make a contribution to the group (verbal or non-verbal), and does not work with the group as a whole and the members themselves to regulate their fear system, exploration of any kind is not going to happen.
4   She had also been encouraged by the past president of the Group Psychotherapy Association of Southern California, Dr Bill Flaxman, in 2004, while presenting her theoretical framework for working with the dynamics of attachment in adult life, to develop a model for group facilitation based on the work she was doing on attachment.

All this led McCluskey to devise a model which would enable her to investigate Heard and Lake's ideas, to see if she could understand them better, and whether they could be useful to clinicians who offered to respond helpfully and knowledgeably to other people.

So, she sent out flyers to hospitals, clinics, social services, and voluntary organizations to see if professional caregivers were interested in exploring the dynamics of attachment in their own adult life.

The flyer read thus:

An Exploration of the Dynamics of Attachment in Adult Life

> *This course seeks to address the fact that as we work in jobs that require us to respond to the needs of others, too often we don't create the conditions to support our own personal and psychological development. Experiences of careseeking and caregiving have their roots in infancy and shape our expectations and responses to careseeking and caregiving in adult life. As professionals offering a service in the field of mental health and social care we will be aware of the many different ways that people express their careseeking needs, and how difficult it is sometimes to interpret these accurately and respond. People who have had contradictory experiences of caregiving will often tend to miscue professional caregivers so that any attempt at caregiving is frustrated and can end up as a frustrating experience for both parties.*
>
> *The dynamics of attachment consist of several goal-corrected systems. These are careseeking, caregiving, sexuality, exploratory interest sharing with peers, the personal system for self-defence, the internal supportive or unsupportive environments and the personally created external supportive environment (home/ lifestyle). The theory suggests that these systems work together as a single*

process to contribute to and maintain maximum well-being. Each session will have a short didactic input on the attachment system to be explored that day, followed by two experiential groups with a short break in between. There will be time to identify what people are learning, discovering or applying to their own practice. Una McCluskey has been researching attachment dynamics for many years and will seek permission from the group to continue this work.

Professional caregivers of all types and theoretical persuasions still respond to this invitation today, and the work that she started is now carried on by people who have attended her courses and training in many centres in Ireland, the UK, Portugal, Sweden, Denmark, the Czech Republic and the USA.

The structure that McCluskey created for this exploration

Nine three-hour sessions, once a month for nine months. Each session focused on one of the core systems within the Restorative Process outlined by Heard and Lake. Therefore, session one focused on careseeking, session two on caregiving, session three of self-defence, session four on interest sharing, session five on sexuality, session six on the internal environment, session seven on the personally created external environment, session eight on how these seven systems interacted within the self, and session nine was a review of the whole course. There was didactic input before each session on the system to be explored that day. After that the participants were encouraged to explore what they knew about this aspect of themselves. The facilitator worked in such a way as to create, as far as possible, a fear-free environment so that exploration could thrive. This involved absolute attention to regulating the affect of the participants and encouraging supportive companionable relating; in other words, constantly addressing and regulating the arousal of the fear system.

So, the structure for each session (following the initial one) was:

1 Backtrack and catch up following the previous month's session. This involved asking the members to bring in anything they could remember from the last session or any discoveries or learning that occurred to them in the time in between.
2 Introduction by the facilitator to the aspect of the self to be explored that day.
3 Experiential work exploring that aspect of the self.
4 Break.
5 Experiential work continued.
6 Application of learning to work settings.
7 Surprises, learnings, and discoveries from the whole session.

There have been exceptions to this structure in that McCluskey has moved to three-day events, as opposed to running the course over nine months. She has also used a different structure while working abroad. Many people who have trained in the McCluskey model are offering these types of courses for professional caregivers and members of the general public who are interested in this type of work in the UK, Ireland, and Portugal. The model is being used with clinical psychology doctoral students in Limerick and Galway as part of their training, and also with students on each year of the four-year training course at the Bowlby Centre in London as part of their training as attachment-based psychoanalytic psychotherapists. The work has been adapted by Nicola Neath for organizational settings (Neath & McCluskey, 2019).

Facilitation of the experiential groups to enable exploration of the dynamics of attachment

McCluskey set up this work to investigate the theory of Heard and Lake, but she also had clear goals for the participants. She invited them to be curious about the idea that the seven systems were different from each other, had separate goals, and that the person experienced different sets of emotions on reaching the goals of different systems; for example, the relief one feels when one's careseeking system is met, or the vitality one experiences when engaged in interest sharing. Getting the hang of this took longer for some participants than others. For some it took a further course or more, but when people did get the experience of reaching the goal of a system they would usually say, and with some vitality, 'now I know what Una was on about when she talked about reaching the goal'.

This meant that members were also beginning to discriminate within themselves which aspect of the self was getting aroused at any one time. For example, was it their caregiving? Caregiving could be aroused in relation to an adolescent son or daughter, but the son or daughter might not cooperate with the form of care being offered, leaving both parties possibly angry or distressed. This is the experience when a system is aroused but is not reaching its goal. For the parent it may be the arousal of caregiving, for the son or daughter it may be the arousal of the system for personal self-defence; or to put it another way, for the parent, the arousal of the caregiving self, for the son or daughter, the arousal of the defensive self.

Another thing she was keen for participants to explore was the difference between the arousal of a system, such as sexuality, and the self. When the person gets the experience that the careseeking self or the sexual self or the defensive self is not the same as the self, they can experience the freedom to think and reflect on what they want and how to resource themselves. This is the paradox of how we experience the self, beautifully articulated by J.D. Sutherland (1993) and by Dorothy Heard (Heard, Lake & McCluskey, 2009/ 12, Chapter Two). We experience the self simultaneously as autonomous and yet embedded in relationships.

Having set out her reasons for exploring the dynamics of attachment in adult life, the model she created to do that, and the hopes she had for what people would get out of it, we now want to explore how McCluskey dealt with transferential phenomena in the group context.

The reader will appreciate that whatever intentions one has for a piece of work, however one describes the purpose of the work, people bring their own expectations to it, most of which will be unknown to the facilitator precisely because of the phenomenon of transference.

Engaging with transference in a group context

First of all, transference is aroused on first meeting whether that is on paper, electronically, voice tone or in person. We are aware that the first group session represents a strange situation and that this context automatically arouses the system for personal defence. Because of this, the first thing we do is centre the group. We ask the group to pay attention to the state they are in, particularly what is happening in their bodies. We ask them to accept the state they are in and to welcome it. We ask them to try to stay in the now and just notice if they are time travelling to the past or the future. We acknowledge that it is a new situation and that the normal and natural state to be in is one of cautious suspicion. We suggest that they should make the most use of that and to keep checking the facilitator and what he or she is up to to make sure they are in a safe environment. We ask them to keep checking this, but also to monitor whether they are being so suspicious they can't take anything in, to try to keep a balance.

Because the focus of the work is to explore one's own dynamics of attachment, this cannot be done if one is acting out of the arousal of one's own caregiving system. I therefore say to the group that in this situation I am the caregiver. I say to them, 'I know you are all caregivers but I am asking you to try to contain yourselves and to notice that, if the facilitator makes a mess of things, see whether he or she notices and makes a repair'. I say to them that, in terms of attachment dynamics and understanding the self better, it is important they try not to act out the arousal of their caregiving selves, as to do so means they are not as free to do their own exploratory work. It is at this point that I say that if they do come to the rescue of someone, I might stop them and this will undoubtedly trigger hurt and anger, and will certainly be experienced as misattunement, but that I am alerting them now to the reason why this might happen.

In order to minimize the arousal of an unsupportive internal environment or the defensive selves of the participants, we say we don't go in for introductions, nobody will be asked to say how far up the professional ladder they are, what their job is or anything else. We say that, in our experience, this arouses fear in everyone and that the whole point of a group like this is to lower the fear level so that exploration can take place in a supportive and companionable environment.

In order to minimize the chance that one member might accidentally become the focus for the group, we say that we won't let anyone talk for more than a couple of minutes to start off with as we are aware that letting one person speak at length puts them in a vulnerable position in the group, which is not good for them and not good for the group.

In order to introduce the idea of supportive companionable relating as opposed to the idea of an isolated self, managing life on their own, we say whatever we are doing we all do it, and wherever we are going we all go together.

In order to impress that this is not a group where anyone needs 'fixing', we say this is not a group where one person explores and the others watch. We affirm that one person's work is work for everyone and that, as one person explores and the facilitator works with them, it is important that the group works along on their own 'lookalikes' to the issue being presented. We affirm that everyone here is here for the same reason, to try to understand themselves a little better. We repeat if it has not been said before that the facilitator will keep to time, and ask that confidentiality be supported and agreed.

In order to minimize the opportunity for the group space itself to trigger the dynamics of disorganization, we create an ordered space. We locate and orientate to time and task. We also say that this work takes place on the edge of the unknown, that it is not prepackaged or prescribed, that the work is to stay in the here and now as much as possible, and that inevitably misattunements will arise in the transferential space.

Feedback from hundreds of participants over the years confirms what an impression this kind of beginning has made on them. They particularly mention the freedom to drop the caregiving role and the invitation not to introduce themselves other than by name alone.

Ongoing work in the group, foreground and background: affect regulation of the member and the group as a whole

We know that from the moment we are born we are seeking contact with another human being like ourselves. Studies of infant behaviour have shown that babies are signalling this intention from the start, sometimes by the tiniest of eye movements. Colwyn Trevarthen (2016) has shown that a five-month-old baby interacting with her mother anticipates by a fraction of a second the phrasing of her mother's voice. This and other studies show that babies are attuned to the people who care for them in a very immediate bodily way and are affected not only by the affect of the other but by that nature of the response they get from the other. One of the points that Ainsworth and her team noticed in the Baltimore study was that the way the mother responded to her six-month-old infant predicted security of attachment at one year.

Taking this into the context of facilitating an exploratory group, I (McCluskey) have made it my practice to respond to every single thing a person says in the group, at least until the group is up and going and self-managing in a balanced way. This means everyone is participating more or less equally and at the same level of intimacy, connection with self, and with each other. I do this by using a word, a brief précis or a tone of voice, but respond is what I do. I also talk to the group as a whole all the time, so that not only am I regulating the affect, pace of speaking, and volume of delivery of the person coming into the group, I am also regulating the group as a whole by constantly reminding them to centre, make space, to stay in the now, not to respond to the desire to fix or make better, but to work at relaxing the tension in their bodies so that the person speaking does not have the extra baggage of attuning to tension and fear in the group – I often add, 'they have enough themselves to cope with'. I use the simple phrase 'tension down everybody'. And I may go on to say, 'just notice … our bodies react to even the mention of the words "fear" or "trauma" or "anger" or "rejection" or "shame"'.

Working with transferential phenomena from the embodied defensive self of one member to the group as a whole

During these courses for practitioners in the caring professions it is inevitable that people will access memories of traumatic events either in relation to how they were treated as children or an intimate assault on their person as children or young adults. Sometimes it is an event that has happened about which they have felt terrified or ashamed. Sometimes it is unprocessed grief. Sometimes a person carries unresolved trauma from having been caught up in a war zone. Trauma presents in many and varied ways. Because these courses are not designed or advertised as providing therapy, another way had to be found to address these major life issues as they emerge as members explore their careseeking, caregiving selves, their defensive and interest sharing selves, and their sexual selves. When these events have been too much to contain and process, they remain for the most part unintegrated and the impact on the person somewhat unknown until triggered in one of the exploratory sessions.

What happens in a group is that members attune to the affect in the room, whether the atmosphere is tense or relaxed. Attuning to fear will arouse tension in the body and certain chemicals will flow. If members in a group automatically attune to the state the traumatized person is in, it is imperative that the facilitator starts to regulate the affect of everyone in the group. Otherwise the person with the trauma is going to attune to the tension in the group and this will inevitably impact on their capacity to freely explore their experience. With profound trauma that has required the person to manage the situation alone and without the help of others, they will have managed by using their mobilization system (fight/flight) or their immobilization system (shut down). These defensive strategies can be easily triggered in a group situation that is left unregulated by the facilitator.

What I have learned to do on these occasions is to ask the group to centre and let the tension go. I say, 'the most important thing you can do now to help X is to centre and be present in the here and now, and let as much tension go as you can. They do not need your tension, they have enough of their own'. I remind them of the power of attunement happening always out of consciousness, in the here and now. I interrupt anyone who is aroused to ask questions of the person with the traumatic memory, and stop them from doing so. I try to do this in as sensitive a way as possible (not always successfully). I ask the group if they support the work that is happening between me and the person with the trauma, and make sure that the person with the memory of trauma has a visual awareness that members of the group are present, focused, and supportive. I do this by asking for a quick look around the group. This often takes the form of a cursory look around the room, but, however fleeting, it is important as a way of helping the person stay centred in the here and now. It is important to counter the impulse to regress to the past.

I then start to work with the person with the memory. I slow the pace down to nearly zero, I ask if the person can access their curiosity. I ask if they want me to work with them. I stay until I am sure the person is responding to me out of curiosity and not submission. I ask if they can be curious about what we might do, and I ask if they have a sense that they can stop the exploration when and if they wish to do so. I ask the group if they can support this. I again ask the person if they can look at the group, however briefly and by skirmish only. I remind them where they are, at this moment, and who they are with. I say to the group that most of our information resides in our bodies and that it is the information in their bodies at this moment that I want them to pay attention to. The reader will notice that this is micro engagement with individual and group process, that it is calling everyone into exploratory mode, to be present and alive to the present.

I call the person who is working into relationship with me not to sink down into the memory of the experience, or do that physically by collapsing their body. I counter the impulse to regress and collapse in every way I can. I ask them to speak as loudly as possible, to notice their physical collapse, to talk through the tears. I work slowly and carefully with the person, validating their experience and saying that I believe them. I say, 'you don't have to re-enact what happened to you, you don't have to go back into the experience. I believe you, just tell me what happened in a good strong voice'. I clarify ambiguity, I track in detail what happened, I keep validating, regulating, and talking to the group as I go. I say to the group it is important to carry on monitoring what is happening in their bodies as they listen. I say this is a group where one person's work is work for everyone.

At a point in the work, when it seems the person working is finished, I turn to the group and ask them if they have any information for the person who was speaking, from what they are experiencing in their bodies. I want body experiences, emotion, not questions, not speculation. I keep asking the group until everyone has had something to say. Usually there is someone who says, 'I just cut off, wasn't involved, didn't get involved'. I usually respond to this by saying this is information for person X and it may well make sense to them. (It makes complete sense to me that they may have attuned to the defence mechanism used by the traumatized person at the time of the assault; i.e., dissociation or immobilization.) I go on to validate their contribution in a robust voice myself and say something like, 'so you didn't get involved and were experiencing being cut off'. I say it in a voice that validates, normalizes, and regulates – there is no criticism, no judgment – but it is clear to me that this may be a very important piece of feedback to the person who is working.

Other responses from the group often include feeling restricted around the throat, pain or turbulence in the tummy, leaden legs, pain in neck, all sorts of sensations all over body parts, including the impulse to lactate or defecate. I keep information from the group strictly to what they are aware of happening in their bodies.

At this point I turn to the central person and ask if they could hear any of that. On all the occasions that this type of work has taken place in the group the person has answered, yes, they could hear. I then ask them to repeat out loud what they heard people say. I then ask if what they heard makes sense to them. It always has. And it is the case that, on all occasions, the person who had been accessing traumatic memories has said they have never experienced anything like this before, they were able to access the past without feeling vulnerable or regressed, that they do not have a sense of needing to talk about this in this way again.

My own sense of what has happened is that the person at last feels their horrific experience has been witnessed, understood, and validated. The fact that members could catch aspects of the experience in their own bodies confirms for the person that what they experienced in their body at the time of the assault has been witnessed and understood and that they are not alone with this anymore. The power of witness is crucial in regulating the aftermath of traumatic experiences: the fact that someone was there and saw what happened. Most times, traumatic experience happens when the person is alone, so this type of work, which focuses on body responses to hearing about the trauma, is the nearest one can get to actually witnessing the original assault. Picking up the experiences in the body happens through being centred and attuned to the state the other is in, being exploratory and not in the grip of one's own system of flight or flight, immobilization, defensive caregiving or anything else.

This is working with transferential phenomena from the embodied defensive self of one member to the group as a whole. It involves working through attunement to one's own body attuning to the body of another.

Sometimes the person with the traumatic memory presents with violent shuddering of their body, with or without sounds of agony and pain. They may be curious why they are shaking suddenly, they may say they have a memory or something will have happened in the group to spark it. If it is clear to me that they are in touch with that memory again now and I am up to a time boundary in the group, I will ask the group if they support breaking the time boundary for an amount of time to stay with what is happening. I haven't always done this in the past. But I now think it is very important if something has spontaneously triggered the affect attached to a memory that one stays with it while it is available to the person and works with it, but within a revised and agreed time boundary.

There are many varied ways in which transferential phenomena manifest in a group. The response of the facilitator takes a similar path to the one just described. One works with the body, one calls people to centre, one amplifies, regulates, and validates. One stays centred and normalizes, and one monitors whether one's own fear system is getting triggered. There have been times when I have been overwhelmed by the strength of the transference and have not been able to respond in a helpful way. That is why it is so important, if one takes on this work, that one has available an explorative caregiver that one can go to to help regulate one's own distress and think things through so that one can emerge, if the situation presents itself again, in a more exploratory, supportive, and companionable state. However, sometimes one has to live with a rupture that never heals.

What have professional caregivers made of the experience of exploring their own attachment dynamics?

Counting just the nine-month, three-day, and one-day courses I have facilitated in Ireland, the UK, Portugal, the USA, Australia and other countries, I have facilitated more than 100 such courses in the past twelve years. In all, 810 people have attended (counting just the nine-month and three-day events), some more than once. Thirty-four nine-month courses have been transcribed by my colleague Jim Gunn (McCluskey & Gunn, 2015). This involved transcribing 637 hours of actual group exploratory time. Three hundred and eighty-three people attended; fifty-six (15%) of these were men and 327 were women (85%). In addition, Gunn has transcribed two five-day courses and one three-day course. All this work is anonymized and participants gave their consent at the time for the sessions to be recorded in the interest of furthering our understanding of the Restorative Process and how it might work in ourselves and in our clients.

As well as drawing on this material I will also draw on the results of a questionnaire I distributed to all those who took my three-day courses in 2011 and 2012, ninety-six people in all. I was interested to check whether my perception of what I would consider a relatively minimal input in terms of exploratory work was indeed having a substantial effect on their life and times, personally and professionally.

The data that I have gathered give us an opportunity to do a couple of things. One is to look at the outcome of the work for the participants who were clearly able to make changes in their professional and personal lives. Second is to look at the way in which trauma can be worked with in a group context.

Because of the vast quantity of data, I can only give a short flavour of what has emerged from this work. The following lists give snapshots of some of what professional caregivers have said about their reasons for becoming caregivers at a very young age.

What I have found is that the arousal of caregiving at a very early age within the family of origin is usually accompanied by the arousal of the personal system for self-defence, in the form of the fear system. As such I tend to refer to this form of caregiving as defensive.

First let us look at the reasons professional caregivers have given for not pursuing care for themselves, the origin of which was often clearly located in childhood experiences.

Barriers against careseeking mentioned by professional caregivers

1   No one there.
2   Fear, panic, and chaos.
3   Feeling stupid.
4   Others' needs are greater.
5   I am the only one that can manage this.
6   Others are not as clever.

As children, professional caregivers had their caregiving selves aroused (alongside their careseeking and their defensive selves) in the family for the following reasons.

Reasons given by professional caregivers for their defensive selves becoming activated

1   To make the world I grew up in a more ordered and safe place.
2   Manage the emotions around feeling vulnerable.
3   No care forthcoming for self.
4   Positive feedback from others.
5   Ill parents.
6   Frightening parents.
7   Siblings to look after.

The main system that is likely to be aroused in these young caregivers is the fear system or the fear aspect of the personal self-defence system. In that way, if the child is successful at regulating their fear by how they have interacted with their caregiver and the response they have got from their caregiver, this will meet the goal of that system (self-defence/fear) and the child will experience temporary relief. But if this is the case, then we are talking about children who then subsequently as adults live out of their fear system. This puts a tremendous strain on their physiological system, in much the way that Stephen Porges has articulated. It is no wonder that in later life these early recruited caregivers experience what they call burnout.

Further exploration in the experiential groups with the professional caregivers elicited that defensive caregiving often impacted other aspects of the self, as shown in the following list.

Defensive caregiving itself a defence against:

1 Intimacy.
2 One's own creativity.
3 Developing and sharing interests with others.
4 Negotiating and resolving home environment.
5 An unsupportive critical internal environment.
6 A supportive internal environment.
7 Building a supportive inner environment.

I have found that it is the exceptional caregiver that has an early life history free from overwhelming fear. In a recent investigation of the transcripts from five different RP courses, Jim Gunn and I (McCluskey & Gunn, 2015) found that 55% of participants had experienced failed careseeking while growing up. What we do not know is whether this is true for the general population or specific to those who go into the caring professions. Comparable study would be worthwhile.

From my exploratory work with professional caregivers I can see that the validation one gets from defensive caregiving, and the positive attributions that accompany it, may help to assuage a deep loneliness in the self, a desire to be seen, a desire to be appreciated as a good person. But the validation achieved through this form of caregiving, tragically, does not support and strengthen the core of the vulnerable self. It is like a drug; the person requires constant access to another fix. This is why it can sometimes look to an outsider and be experienced by the person themselves as 'compulsive caregiving'. Defensive caregiving can also support the process of excluding from consciousness those experiences, emotions, and attributions that are both painful to the self and unsupportive of the self. To this extent, the person may be in complete denial that they are in the grip of these dynamics. Their sense of themselves and their self-esteem may be boosted by belonging to a profession held in high social esteem.

When we move into defensive caregiving we lose our freedom, we have no degree of freedom other than to respond to the demands of the other. It is a process that is driven by fear, consciously or otherwise. The consequences of not responding are not thought about, sometimes cannot be thought about, and the impact on others can be terrible.

Clients can threaten the well-being of therapists. We do not often talk about this fact. When this happens the therapist's own fear system is likely to be triggered, as is their attachment system, expressed through careseeking. The therapist's internal environment will be aroused and will be either supportive or unsupportive in regulating their fear system. If their internal environment is supportive, it will remind them of their competence and enable them to take an exploratory stance towards the presentation of the careseeker, perceived initially as a threat. If the therapist is not able to access an internal or external supportive environment then they are likely to move into a defensive response. When this takes the form of caregiving infiltrated by fear (defensive caregiving), it can have dire consequences for carer and cared for alike.

Defensive caregiving is what a person may resort to when they are not met as a person, not seen as a person, their needs left unattended, left abandoned and alone, sometimes in terrible pain and distress, sometimes bored. As mentioned earlier in the book, when one's needs are overridden by an adult caregiver it is usual for the adult to accompany their non-verbal aggression, lack of response, or dismissiveness by some verbal attribution – most normally of a negative kind: 'How could you be so demanding – can you not just leave me alone?' 'You are such a nuisance.' These attributions, as Dorothy Heard has pointed out, very often become core beliefs of the self and contribute to an unsupportive internal environment. So, it is possible that at the core of the unmet self we have a very harsh or vicious internal environment where the person may believe they are unwelcome in the world and not truly loved for his or her self.

When a person is under threat they can respond and act out of one or the other of these primary biological goal-corrected systems, fear or careseeking. Both will get activated. It is a question of which one will determine the person's behaviour. The outcome of the dynamic interaction between these systems is central to the thesis being presented in this chapter. The behaviour of fear will lead to potentially sadistic, masochistic, freeze or disorganized behaviour; the behaviour of careseeking offers the potential to the person of having their feelings of threat and fear assuaged and being offered some skills and support to figure out how to cope, provided they can discern and approach the presence of an exploratory caregiver who is not in the grip of their own fear system.

The work that I have been doing with professional caregivers is not about identifying attachment patterns. It is an in-depth exploration of what they know about what activates careseeking in the here and now, how they express it, and whether they experience being met and what that feels like in the body.

We look at the whole process of how the various systems work together to maintain levels of well-being and whether, in fact, well-being is restored or not, given the behaviour of the person and the responses of others. It is this understanding that the therapists then bring to their work with clients. So, it is very different indeed to simply naming one's attachment pattern.

It is helping therapists of all persuasions to centre in the here and now; to respect the information they get in their bodies through the process of attuning to the affect of others. Recognizing the power of affect attunement and attunement to the body state of the other, caregivers can begin to explore the effect on their own development of attuning to the affect of fearful, frightening, dismissive, neglectful or very tense and stressed early caregivers. The work emphasizes exploration over interpretation, validates the reality of people's past and present experience, supports their competence to have survived so far with well-being, and focuses on what one can do now to change their pattern of careseeking so that people might get access to more effective caregiving. This is the driver for change.

One of my findings from the groups for professional caregivers is the vast number of people who can identify when their caregiving system was first aroused. In many cases the other system that was aroused in parallel to their caregiving was the flight/fight/freeze aspect of their defensive selves, often aroused in relation to ill, distressed, distracted, dysfunctional or disturbed parent figures. Many have known from a very young age that, in order to get any attention at all, they needed to submit to their caregiver and do their bidding. They were also often expected to offer empathy and care to their would-be caregiver. So, we have the arousal of the caregiving system and the arousal of the fear system at the same time. Very often the child was attuning to the fear of the adult and trying to regulate the adult as best they could through providing care, but the whole situation, of course, was too big for the child to manage and what got lost was the child him/herself and any awareness by an adult that the child was dysregulated and trying to cope with something that was too much for them.

The legacy of Bowlby's work for the 21st century is, in my view, the need to support our professional caregivers, provide opportunities for them to expand their consciousness of themselves, help them to connect with their biological selves, and help them to become better careseekers. All of this so that they can grow and develop through their interactions with effective caregivers, who can moderate their caregiving in order to make space for an interest sharing life. Defensive caregiving seems to wipe out any possibility of allowing space for a self to develop, a self that would find itself through exploring its own interests and developing its own life.

We need to support the development of a living process that is operating in the here and now, using information from our bodies to access whether our own fear system has become aroused by feeling threatened by our clients or by the activation of our own unsupported internal environment. We need to regulate that system for ourselves so that we can remain truly exploratory with our clients.

The model that I have developed to do this I have called 'exploratory goal-corrected psychotherapy' (EGCP). The nature of this model can be seen in Michael's work in Chapters Four and Five. The model has come from the map that I have been using with professional caregivers to explore the biological systems within themselves that interact to enable them to maintain as much well-being as possible. The work of the facilitator is to enable the person(s) to identify what system is aroused in the here and now and to interact with them in such a way that the person experiences reaching the goal of that system. In that way the work for the person is exploring goal-corrected systems and the work of the facilitator is itself goal-corrected. If the facilitator fails to reach the person, misses them, or becomes fearful in response to them, the interaction is not goal-corrected; both remain distressed and development does not proceed on the basis of core support at the centre of the self, trans-forming and strengthening the self.

When a great deal of a person's life is taken up in caregiving to others, it is important to listen out for the way they talk about this fact, their energy levels, their vitality, their hopes and fears for their own well-being, and the effect of this behaviour on other aspects of their life and times. It may well be a source of great satisfaction to them and what gives most meaning to their lives. It may be important to explore with them whether the way they offer care to another is from an empathic base fuelled by curiosity and exploration and whether they experience being able to meet the needs of that person, thereby (in biological terms) meeting the goals of their caregiving self. When this is not the case we may be in the territory of unmet careseeking mas-querading as caregiving.

This is careful, delicate work. If a person changes their behaviour to family, friends, and others and no longer is the person everyone can rely on to run, fetch, and do everyone's bidding, they may well face a backlash. They may find themselves ostracized and abandoned. They may no longer be welcome at family gatherings and celebrations and they may also get flak at work for not taking on as much work as before. When a person's identity, self-esteem, status in their world, their well-being, and their sense of belonging is enme-shed in caregiving, then all those issues need to be explored with the person as they change the dynamic of their internal organization. This can only be done with an increased capacity to careseek and a corresponding capacity to dis-criminate who to seek care from as they go forward with their life.

What is clearly needed now going forward is a much more detailed under-standing of who goes into the caring professions, what sort of experiences in childhood they have had, and what are their vulnerabilities to practising defensively or becoming burnt out. How do their early experiences of attach-ment relationships influence their capacity to co-operate effectively with other caregivers? Lack of professional co-operation, communication, and under-standing has been cited in numerous reports and enquiries as the root cause of failure to adequately protect children and vulnerable adults (Department for Education, 2008; Department of Health, 2004; Independent Inquiry into Child Sexual Abuse, 2015). To what extent can this be linked and understood within an attachment frame?

What do we know about the dynamics of attachment of those who offer to take professional responsibility for the care of others? A study of the early experiences of those who go into the 'caring' professions would be useful to us in terms of helping us understand the nature of the task and the vulnerabilities and needs of those who undertake it. Why have we, as a society, given this so little priority? Even as professionals, those in the research end of the business seem to spend endless time refining categories of insecurity in children in relation to caregivers, when spending some of that time studying the dynamics of caregiving, the other end of that two-person, goal-corrected behavioural system – careseeking and caregiving – might be absolutely vital to the well-being of our society as a whole. While Bowlby concentrated on the degree of proximity between careseeker and caregiver, in terms of gauging levels of security and exploration for the child, Dorothy Heard, his consultant colleague for twenty years, concentrated on the nature of the interaction between caregiver and child and whether it was sufficient to return them to the state of exploratory play. Later, Heard et al. (2009/12) developed the concept of caregiving and discriminated between effective and ineffective caregiving.

Effective caregiving was defined as having four functions.

1   To remain exploratory towards the needs of the careseeker and not become defensive themselves in relation to the presentation of the careseeker.
2   To correctly identify the affect of the careseeker and to regulate it.
3   To identify the skills necessary to manage the threatening situation and help the careseeker acquire them.
4   To put the careseeker in touch with their peers (Heard et al., 2009/12).

Ineffective caregiving, on the other hand, is defensive by nature.

Evidence that an increase in effective careseeking is crucial to shift the dynamic of defensive caregiving can be seen from the following study. This was the questionnaire mentioned earlier that was issued to ninety-six participants of my courses. We got sixty-four replies, which represents a 67% return rate.

Significant positive correlations were found between items assessing awareness of the impact of caregiving on well-being ('I am more aware of the effect on my well-being of how I give care to others') and changes in caregiving (i.e., 'I have made changes in the way I give care'; $r = 0.64$, $p < 0.001$). Likewise, an increase in awareness of fear and its impact on the self ('I am aware of that [fear] beginning to change and that I am now less anxious') was also significantly correlated with changes in caregiving ($r = 0.67$, $p < 0.001$).

Thus an increase of changes in caregiving has been associated with increased awareness of the impact of caregiving on fear and well-being, thereby suggesting a shift in defensive caregiving. In terms of seeking care, an increase in awareness of how one seeks care from others when in distress ($r = 0.56$, $p < 0.001$), and awareness of what has made seeking care problematic ($r = 0.49$, $p < 0.001$), were significantly correlated with perceived changes in seeking care, such that increases in awareness of how one seeks care when in distress and how careseeking has been problematic in the past are associated with more changes in careseeking. More research is necessary to support these promising findings.

The questionnaire also asked respondents to rate their agreement with a series of statements and to provide examples of changes resulting from their participation on the course. Seventy-nine per cent had changed the way they sought care from others, with examples including: 'I am more direct and straightforward in the way I ask for help, and less defensively aggressive.' Eighty-nine per cent were more aware of help being available when under stress: 'More able to know when to step back or take a break. More open in supervision.' These changes in careseeking were reflected in 82% of respondents who had made changes in the way they gave care, citing examples such as: 'I am much more aware of my own fear system and the importance of grounding myself if my fear system is activated.'

Seventy-six per cent of those who responded reported changes to interest sharing, such as:

> I am giving myself guilt-free permission to explore what it is I think I'd like and engage with that interest

and

> I have made it more of a priority in my life and feel less guilty for spending money and time on exploring interests that are not directly associated with my work or family commitments.

Thus this research illustrates changes in caregiving, careseeking, and interest sharing. While these are important findings, more research is necessary to illustrate the underlying mechanisms of change during a Restorative Process programme.

The professional caregivers referred to in this chapter have come from a great variety of backgrounds and training, such as psychology, psychiatry, general medicine, paediatrics, social work, teaching, nursing (clinical and administrative), law (both solicitors and barristers), art therapy, psychoanalysis, psychotherapy from many schools of training, counsellors, probation officers, religious (priests from both the Catholic and Anglican tradition), occupational therapy, palliative care, housing, and many others.

We need to work out how we can support those in our society who take on the work of caring. We need to work out how we enable them to thrive in this situation. We will not help our fellow human beings who wish to provide good caring services to others by threatening them, by increasing their levels of fear, and by continuously monitoring and auditing what they are doing. We need to pay attention to the impact of the work on them and how the work they are doing is making them feel inside themselves. Not to treat them like this is to treat them as less than human. We cannot have people we treat as less than human as our main caregivers. What kind of care are we expecting?

Chapter 9

Locating exploratory goal-corrected psychotherapy (EGCP)

A new model of attachment-based practice within the tradition of Fairbairnian object relations and the neuroscience relational psychotherapy of today

In the preface to the first of his trilogy on attachment, John Bowlby states that:

> the field I had started out to plough so light-heartedly was no less than the one Freud had started tilling sixty years earlier … What had deceived me was that my furrows had been started from a corner, diametrically opposed to the one at which Freud had entered, and through which analysts have always followed.
>
> (Bowlby, 1969, p. xi)

We continue to plough from the same furrow as Bowlby, and often find ourselves diametrically opposed to where the rest of attachment theory has gone. We have developed a different developmental line to what Holmes (2009) describes as the 'Ainsworth-Main-Fonagy developmental line' (p. 490). We have followed the 'Bowlby-Heard and Lake-McCluskey developmental line', retaining the concept of 'goal-corrected biologically based interpersonal behavioural systems' and the effects on the self when the goal of these different systems are reached or not, as the basis of our theoretical framework and clinical approach. However, in preparing this chapter we have found that the field in which we are ploughing is occupied by many other participants from many other areas of science.

These new participants – which come from many different disciplines, such as affective neuroscience, neurobiology, and developmental neuroscience – and others have helped us to see what a realignment and reintegration of what both Freud and Bowlby set out to achieve might look like, when they entered the same field of investigation.

In this chapter we give an overview of this field as we now look at it, and locate our particular model of therapy within Fairbairnian object relations, attachment theory, developmental psychology, and neuroscience.

Object relations

Fairbairn (1952) placed the desire for human contact at the heart of the developmental and therapeutic enterprise in a way that was radical at the time. In his 1941 paper Fairbairn states that, 'It would appear as if the point had now been reached at which, in the interests of progress, the classic libido theory would have to be reformed into a theory of development based essentially upon object relations' (Fairbairn, 1941, p. 31). In this one sentence, Fairbairn completes his break from Freud; the departure from classic Freudian analysis of hydraulic energy emanating from the unconscious seeking discharge was complete, and the need to satisfy our instinctual drives of sex and aggression was no longer the only way to view human motivation or behaviour. The role of object relations and the need for contact with another human being from birth were seen as paramount from this moment on.

Needless to say, the implication of such a revision of how human behaviour is viewed is only now being taken on board fully, even in psychotherapy circles. Jeremy Hazell (2000) points out that Fairbairn 'himself predicted that his theory would have far-reaching implications for therapeutic practice, and these areas are still being explored by contemporary writers such as Bollas (1987), Gomez (1997), Scharff (1995), Symington (1986)' (Hazell, 2000, p. 25). However, the proliferation of the object relationships tradition, coupled with the fact that no known school was established as an umbrella for the various proponents of the approach, makes it easy to lose sight of the common ground shared among all object relations theorists, and stems directly from Fairbairn's theory of object relations that 'the ultimate aim of libido is the object' (Fairbairn, 1941, p. 31).

Hazell reminds us that the development of Fairbairn's theory of object relations did not develop out of nowhere, but was grounded in extensive study and detailed analysis of many schizoid patients, like many of the men O'Toole described earlier. In 1940 Fairbairn wrote 'Schizoid factors in the Personality', which Scharff and Birtles describe as 'the first of the truly original papers … which suddenly marked a new path for analytic thought.… The new psychoanalytic path received its orientation by the way Fairbairn put the infant and child's need for a relationship at the centre of development' (Scharff & Birtles, 1994, p. x). This contradiction, that Fairbairn's theory of object relations emerged out of the detailed study of many schizoid patients for whom relations with others are characterized by considerable difficulty, is testimony to the view that, for those for whom emotional connection is most sought after, it is often defended against by the denial and repression of that need. 'In the case of those with whom the schizoid tendency is marked, defence against emotional loss gives rise to repression of affect and an attitude of detachment which leads others to regard them as remote and in more extreme cases even as inhuman' (Fairbairn, 1940, p. 15). It is this contradiction that requires us to ask what has happened to these individuals, and to keep asking that question with the infant and child's need for relationship remaining at the centre of our enquiry.

Fairbairn offered a unique theoretical framework from which we could understand the retreat from verbal interaction into silence and/or the repression of affect. Through his observations of people with schizoid characteristics he noted a tendency for them 'to treat libidinal objects as a means of satisfying their own requirements rather than as persons possessing inherent value' (Fairbairn, 1952, p. 13). In this Fairbairn was getting behind the facade of how people present on the surface and recognizing their inability to use the interaction with the analyst (or caregiver) because of the original lack of response of the primary carers to the infant. Unless the caregiver is able to get beyond the surface presentation and meet the needs of the person seeking contact, which are there from birth, no progress can be made.

Fairbairn saw this 'largely as a regressive phenomenon determined by unsatisfactory emotional relationships with parents and particularly their mothers at a stage in childhood subsequent to the early oral phase in which this orientation begins. The type of mother who is specially prone to provoke such a reaction is the mother who fails to convince her child by spontaneous and genuine expression of affection that she herself loves him as a person' (Fairbairn, 1940, p. 13). We acknowledge that nowadays one would not privilege the mother in the frame in this way. Fairbairn's work predates the work of the developmental psychologists, who have shown the complex dynamic interplay between attachment dynamics in the caregiver (male or female) to the infant as well as the impact of the infant's and the caregiver's own constitution, health, and well-being.

Our own understanding of the unique impact of the first relationship is also influenced by the work of the developmental psychologists, particularly Daniel Stern (1985), Gergely (1996), Trevarthen and Hubley (1978) and Meltzoff and Moore (1977, 1983). Gergely (1996) provides a bridge from the world of psychoanalysis to the world of observation and experiment and provides evidence that non-verbal infants are 'aware of lack of congruence between the affect being displayed on a person's face and the emotion that they are experiencing' (McCluskey, 2005, p. 35). This is what Fairbairn was writing about in his papers in the 1940s and 1950s from his work with schizoid patients.

O'Toole has observed that many of his male clients from the west coast of Ireland are not aware of the need to enter into a relationship with another person in order to change their behaviour. They do not realize that a lack of emotional relating to another person is often at the heart of their interpersonal difficulties. This disconnect between how one presents and what one needs and seeks is often unknown to the person, and this is one of the challenges of this type of work and why the work of Fairbairn makes complete sense even in today's world.

Paul Renn, a psychoanalytic psychotherapist with a background in the National Probation Service in London, developed a particular interest in working with violent men and couples from an attachment and research perspective. In his introduction to his 2012 book, 'The Silent Past and the Invisible Present',

Renn states that he is particularly interested 'in the silent, invisible processes deriving from the past that maintain non-optimal ways of experiencing and relating in the present' (Renn, 2012, pp. xxxiii–xxxiv).

According to Renn, 'earlier clinical models emphasised a largely verbal, interpretative technique in the explicit domain, newer models focus on a nonverbal, affective understanding of communication in the implicit/enactive domain'. He makes the point that 'therapeutic change consists of a dual process and needs to proceed in both of these domains' (Renn, 2012, p. xxxiv). We would contend that the model and practice we present here supports these views. Kirkwood acknowledges what he learned from Graham Clarke, that 'Ronald Fairbairn wished to call his unique development of object relations theory "personal relations theory"' (Clarke 2003 in Kirkwood, 2005, p. 36). Both Fairbairn and Sutherland were deeply influenced by the Scottish philosopher John MacMurray, who describes the concept of the personal as 'primarily the field in which we know one another as persons in personal relations' (MacMurray, 1961, p. 38).

In a clear and lucid account of the 'personal relations theory', Clarke (2005) suggests that the one person that provides a link between MacMurray and Fairbairn is their Scottish contemporary Ian Suttie, who was still active at the time when both men were formulating their later thinking (Clarke, 2005, p. 212). J.D. Sutherland, who first studied psychology, worked in the department of psychology in the University of Edinburgh with MacMurray and Fairbairn in the 1930s. He underwent a personal analysis with Fairbairn before training as a medical doctor in order to fulfil the requirement to train as a psychoanalyst, which he later did in London.

Sutherland was appointed medical director of the Tavistock Clinic in London in 1948 and held that post until he retired in 1966. While at the Tavistock he was one of the few analysts who kept a friendship with John Bowlby and supported his work. Jock, as he was widely known among friends and colleagues, had a wide knowledge of the analytic field both in the UK, Europe, and the USA as editor of the International Journal of Psychoanalysis and later the International Review of Psychoanalysis. He was also keen to return to his native town, Edinburgh. Dr Douglas Haldane, then consultant child and family psychiatrist in Fife amongst others at the Royal Edinburgh Hospital, secured a post which enabled Sutherland to return to Scotland and set up the Scottish Institute of Human Relations (SIHR). His idea was to provide analytic training in individual and group analysis so the information from this specialized field could be made available to those in the wider community of professionals working in health and social services.

Sutherland is a key link in the Scottish object relations tradition. McCluskey trained with Sutherland in the early 1970s and was deeply influenced by his approach and his elucidation of Fairbairnian theory. In fact, she named her 2005 book 'To be Met as Person' having heard Jock give such a title to a paper he gave in 56 Albany Street, Edinburgh, home of the SIHR, in the mid 1970s.

Colin Kirkwood, a contemporary of McCluskey at the SIHR, in his chapter entitled 'The persons-in-relation perspective: Sources and synthesis' (Kirkwood, 2005), provides us with a synthesis of the work of these three great twentieth-century Scotsmen; MacMurray, Suttie, and Fairbairn. In this chapter Kirkwood pulls the different strands of our lineage together in a way that allows us to link our current practice of exploratory psychotherapy right back to the Fairbairnian idea that we are person-seeking from birth. Kirkwood acknowledges Dorothy Heard, niece of Ian Suttie, for 'her painstaking excavations and lucid account of Suttie's life and ideas' in her preface to the 1988 reprinted edition of his book 'The origins of love and hate'. He goes on to summarize Suttie's key contributions:

> What goes on between people, for Suttie is more than the satisfaction of appetites.
>
> Suttie sees the baby as seeking relationships from the start of life, bringing with it the power and will to love, a love which has a special quality of tenderness, embodied in the devoted, loving ministrations of the mother, and the reciprocal emotion of tenderness in the infant. This loving tenderness requires for its satisfaction the awakening of an adequate response of appreciation on the part of the other. Enjoyment, appreciation, and company are sought on both sides, this is the interpersonal context in which bodily needs arise and are met.
>
> (Kirkwood, 2005, p. 26)

In his paper on the autonomous self, Sutherland (1993) puts the nature of this phenomenon as follows: 'Meeting the bodily needs for food does not necessarily keep the baby alive. There is a hunger for stimulating exchanges with the caretaker that must be satisfied to foster a vital dynamic to go on living.'

This work of highlighting the innate need for companionship embodied in love and tenderness of the infant, with the awakening of an adequate response on the part of the other, is also a precursor to the evidence found in the video analysis of the mother-infant interactions which became the stock in trade of the developmental psychologists, such as the work of Meltzoff and Moore (1977, 1983), Meltzoff (1999), Murray and Trevarthen (1985, 1986), Murray (1998), Stern (1977), Beebe and McCrorie (2010), Beebe and Lachmann (2014) and Trevarthen (2016).

Stern video-taped many mother/infant pairs at two, four, six, nine, eighteen, twenty-four, and thirty-six months. He found that on showing these tapes to new or experienced students they were inevitably struck by 'the sense that the two individuals are conducting their interpersonal business in a similar and recognisable fashion throughout' (Stern, 1985, p. 186, in McCluskey, 2005, p. 43). See Trevarthen's (2016) work on musicality between babies and their mothers as further evidence of the dynamic exchange happening at a nonverbal and preverbal level.

It was while viewing the perturbation studies by Lynne Murray (Murray & Trevarthen, 1985, 1986; and Murray, 1998) that McCluskey began to see how these studies could have a direct application to the field of adult psychotherapy. This led her to exploring affect attunement and missattunement in adult psychotherapy (McCluskey, Roger & Nash, 1997). 'Perturbation studies show that infants are distressed when "out of contact" with a person with whom they have been experiencing pleasurable affective experience' (McCluskey, 2005, p. 43). It was through exposure to the work of developmental psychologists, particularly the work of Daniel Stern, that McCluskey's interest in applying what she was noticing and learning from the studies of mother-infant interactions, by slowing down the process to second by second units of interaction through the use of video analysis, could be transferred to a study of therapist-client dyadic interactions. It was this interest in applying the use of video analysis to view the therapeutic interaction in the adult domain that led to McCluskey's discovery of the process of interaction which she conceptualized as goal-corrected empathic attunement (McCluskey, Hooper & Bingley Miller, 1999). At that point she had realized that the process of interaction could be understood within an attachment framework and that, when effective, could be described as 'goal-corrected' within the definition of how instinctive systems worked as described by Bowlby. It is this synthesis of a strong analytic object relations background with an interest and knowledge of video analysis through her work as a family therapist that brings this integration to the forefront of our current practice in both individual and group psychotherapy.

Kirkwood makes the point that:

> the process of repressing on tenderness does not occur in the individual child/mother relationship alone. It has its cultural origin in the stoicism which has pervaded British culture and British Christianity … The process is reinforced beyond the family, particularly among men and boys.
>
> (Kirkwood, 2005, pp. 28–29)

O'Toole argues that the particular form of Catholicism that was dominant in Ireland for centuries and is only now being questioned and abandoned by many in Irish society, together with its very paternalistic culture, which pervaded many aspects of Irish society and Irish family life, has contributed to this taboo on tenderness, especially in many of the men who present for help, but only as a last resort (O'Toole, 2019).

Suttie's contribution anticipates

> much of what comes after, including the work of Fairbairn, Winnicott, Bowlby, Guntrip, Sutherland, the developmental psychologists, our contemporary interest in attunement and attachment, and the more recent contribution of neuroscientists such as Anthony Damasio, who stresses

the importance of internal representation of self and other in human relationships, and the vital role of emotions.

(Damasio, 2000, in Kirkwood, 2005, p. 32; and Damasio, 2018)

Heard and Lake consider 'that Guntrip's description of how to relate therapeutically to a client matches, in large measure, our understanding of companionable supportive caregiving' (Heard & Lake, 1997, p. 136). It is difficult to give a historical account of the development of object relations theory and to show how our practice may differ from the earlier theorists. Unlike them, we have access to research and knowledge about human development and interaction based on very detailed microanalysis of interaction.

In many cases the difference between then and now may be just a question of language. In Guntrip's work on the withdrawn, or repressed, ego, which he saw as having given up on all relationships either external or internal in a symbolic return to prenatal life, where there are no objects separate from the self, we would redraw and describe that within an attachment frame. From this perspective we would see the careseeking self of the infant and the caregiving self of the adult both infiltrated by their systems for self-defence, leading to the state of profound withdrawal in one or both.

In Guntrip's view:

> the ultimate aim of psychotherapy is to enable those who need to do so to surrender to the pull of the regressed ego and allow total dependence on the therapist, returning gradually to relationship as a whole being, under her protection and understanding.
>
> (Gomez, 1997, p. 142)

In our model we don't support the idea of regression. In attachment terms it is important that the caregiving provided by the caregiver remains exploratory. They may need access to an exploratory caregiver themselves to support this happening. With such support, the caregiver, while attuning to the distress of the careseeker, supports the person in distress to return to an exploratory state within themselves through keeping their connection with the caregiver. This can involve calling them into relationship with you as the caregiver, attending to their posture, and encouraging them to notice if they are experiencing a postural collapse. We actively counter the impulse to regress by encouraging the person to centre, speaking in a loud, solid, and clear voice, and thereby discouraging a re-enactment as described in the last chapter.

McCluskey shows how quickly a person can be facilitated to move from a place of defence into the relational, with an accurate empathic response from the caregiver. She describes how she counters the impulse to regress to a re-enactment of the original trauma.

It is Guntrip's account of his analysis with both Fairbairn and Winnicott, which he describes in his 1975 paper 'My experience of analysis with Fairbairn and

Winnicott (How complete a result does psycho-analytic therapy achieve?)', that gives us a unique insight into an analytic experience (Guntrip, 1975). Guntrip describes Fairbairn as sticking to his Freudian analysis despite his theoretical achievements, while he describes Winnicott as 'coming right into the emptiness of my "object relations situation" in infancy with a non-relating mother' (Guntrip, 1975, p. 461). He was, of course, referring to his mother's lack of availability to him following the death of her son, Guntrip's brother.

Brian Lake, who went on to develop the theory of attachment-based exploratory interest sharing (TABEIS) with Dorothy Heard, was deeply influenced by the work of Guntrip, who was his training analyst. Lake went on to make a major contribution to our understanding of the psychoanalytic concept 'ego-strength' by showing how 'ego-strength' was uniquely connected with the development of social and interpersonal competence (Lake, 1985). This observation turned out to be a major cornerstone in the theory he and Heard went on to develop. When all the systems within the dynamics of attachment function optimally, there is no doubt that social and interpersonal competence is vastly increased.

'Psychoanalytic therapy is not like a technique of the experimental sciences, an objective thing-in-itself working automatically. It is a process of interaction, a function of two variables, the personalities of two people working together towards free spontaneous growth' (Guntrip, 1975, p. 465). In this Guntrip foresees the work of McCluskey (1999, 1997, 2005) in her account of this process of interaction in adult dyadic psychotherapy.

This process of interaction (GCEA) 'locates caregiving in the psychotherapeutic context within the theory of the dynamics of attachment (Heard & Lake, 1997). The process I am describing is active and interactional, it is a process of communicating and regulating vitality affects' (McCluskey, 2005, p. 77).

We place our work within its historical context; the authors themselves have been influenced by the psychoanalytic tradition which reaches back to Fairbairn, Guntrip, Winnicott, and Bowlby, and with detailed knowledge of both Freud and Kleinian psychodynamic theory. O'Toole had several years' supervision with Dorothy Heard and has ongoing supervision with Susan Vas Dias. The practice which we call exploratory goal-corrected psychotherapy (EGCP) is based on psychotherapy as a process of interaction which seeks to ensure that the goals of the seven aspects of the self described by Heard and Lake reach their goal.

We will now look at some of the evidence emanating from the neurobiology studies over the past years that provide support from a neurological perspective for many of the hypothesis underpinning our theoretical and clinical work.

Neuroscience and psychotherapy

In his book 'The Science of the Art of Psychotherapy' (2012), Allan Schore states that 'A fundamental principle of my work is that any developmental theory must integrate psychology with biology' (Schore, 2012, p. 1). What Schore is suggesting is 'the concept of modern attachment/regulation theory as an amalgam of Bowlby's attachment theory, updated object relations theories, self-psychology, and contemporary relational theory – all informed by neuroscience and infant research' (Schore, 2012, p. 45). It is this bridging of new science and old theories and clinical practice gained over more than a century now that places exploratory goal-corrected psychotherapy at the leading edge of modern psychotherapy practice.

Deb Dana, a leading neuroscientist who has worked with Stephan Porges (2001, 2007) on making the polyvagal theory developed by Porges more user friendly and understandable, explains that the polyvagal theory is not a treatment modality in itself. It is a model, an approach that sits underneath all the other ways we have been trained in, giving it a foundation, a platform. What the neuroscience revolution offers is the biological underpinning of many of our 'pearls of wisdom' gleaned from our clinical practices and theoretical conceptualizations to date. 'By drawing on a wide range of independent branches of science from neurobiology to attachment we can deepen our understanding of human experience and the art of psychotherapy' (Siegel, 2003, p. 1).

In 2001 Schore was invited to give the Seventh Annual John Bowlby Lecture. In this talk Schore argues that 'The most significant psychoanalytic contributor to our understanding of developmental processes was, indeed, John Bowlby (Schore, 2000a, b) ... he (Bowlby) applied then current biology to a psychoanalytic understanding of infant-mother bonding, and in so doing offered his "Project", an attempt to produce a natural science of developmental psychology' (Schore, 2003a, p. 11). Schore further suggests that 'the great advances in our knowledge of early development have been the engine which has transformed contemporary psychoanalysis' (Schore, 2003a, p. 11).

> We now know that the infant functions in a fundamentally unconscious way, and unconscious processes in an older child or adult can be traced back to the primitive functioning of the infant. Knowledge of how the maturation of the right brain, 'the right mind', is directly influenced by the attachment relationship offers us a chance to more deeply understand, not just the contents of the unconscious but its origins, structure, and dynamics.
>
> (Schore, 2003a, p. 12)

Complementing this, according to Schore, 'the neurobiological aspects of attachment theory allow for a deeper understanding of how an affect-focused developmentally oriented treatment can alter internal structure within the patient's brain/mind/body system' (Schore, 2003a, p. 13).

What is becoming clear from all of the research from neuroscience is that, in order to assuage the arousal of the careseeker, the caregiver has to operate from a fear-free place of empathic exploratory caregiving, where they are active, responsive, and interested in helping the careseeker. We have many ways of describing when the caregiver is not attuned to the needs of the infant, child or adult, but our language often does not capture easily the state required of the caregiver to provide effective care. To do this the caregiver needs to be fully grounded in their body. They need to be communicating from what Porges calls their social engagement system, the myelinated circuit of the vagus nerve. In this state our heart rate is regulated, our breath is full, we have access to a supportive internal environment, and we are competent in our ability to provide care.

Janina Fisher (2017), in her article 'Twenty-five years of trauma treatment: What have we learned?', states very honestly that, 'Counter to my training and practice over twenty years I learned to interrupt clients to ensure that they did not become dysregulated and overwhelmed, and not only did I get to talk, I no longer felt bound to listen silently. Instead I learned to make vocal responses to the client's narrative – 'Hmm … Yes … Uh-ha … Brilliant …' (Fisher, 2017, p. 282). Fisher goes on to say that 'Interrupting, and remaining in vocal contact for example was meant to not only help the client feel "met" but also to regulate autonomic arousal and keep the prefrontal cortex online' (p. 282). The caregiver of the infant, child or adult has to remain within the ventral vagal pathway of the parasympathetic nervous system. This is a bio-logical fact which supports our intuitive understanding of effective caregiving.

Fisher's discoveries from clinical work and her training with Pat Ogden (2006) in sensorimotor psychotherapy are echoed by McCluskey in her dis-coveries from her work in exploratory groups with caregivers (McCluskey, 2007, 2008, 2015), her research into the dynamics of interaction in adult psychotherapy (McCluskey, 2001, 2005), and her training in systems-centred group psychotherapy with Yvonne Agazarian, who in turn had been influ-enced by Davenloo's short-term dynamic psychotherapy (Agazarian, 1997).

When the caregiver interrupts the flow of the narrative to access the affec-tive experience of the careseeker, this triggers the early experience of mis-attunement from the primary attachment figure in relation to which their current presentation is a defence. It is important that the caregiver remains aware of the careseeker's response to their misattunement and the careseeker's non-verbal signals of withdrawal, anger or despair in order that whatever repair is necessary can be achieved so that the relationship remains open and exploratory. This is a complex and fluid process.

As Schore (2003) reminds us, 'for the mother or caregiver to be able to perform this function s/he needs to be in a psychological and biological fear free state of exploration. The key to this is the caregiver's capacity to monitor and regulate her own affect, especially negative affect' (Schore, 2003a, p. 16).

Therefore 'the mother's psychobiological attunement to the infant's arousal and psychobiological state occurs in nonverbal communications of eyes, faces, voice prosody (infant directed speech) and touch, and in such bodily based transactions she intuits what the infant feels, and needs at the moment. Attuned sensitivity of caregivers is amply supported by research as being the one factor consistently associated with secure attachment (Ainsworth, Blehar, Waters & Wall, 1978; De Wolff & Van IJzendoorn, 1997; Van IJzendoorn & De Wolff, 1997)' (Schore, 2012, pp. 397–398).

In 1997 Heard and Lake wrote, 'should caregivers fail to meet the needs of careseekers, the latter cannot experience the goal of careseeking and commonly become frustrated and then depressed. What happens when each partner is failing to reach their goals and what is happening to their respective caregiving and careseeking systems is increasingly being researched and understood in both non-humans and human beings' (Heard & Lake, 1997, p. 5). We now have this research at hand through the work of Schore (2012), Ogden, Minton and Pain (2006), Porges (2001, 2007), Beebe et al. (2010), Beebe and Lachmann (2014), McCluskey, Hooper and Bingley Miller (1999) and McCluskey (2001, 2005).

We will now focus on the work of Beebe and Lachmann (2014). Working from a dyadic systems approach (Beebe, Jaffe & Lachmann, 1992; Jaffe et al., 2001; Beebe & Lachmann, 2003; Beebe, Knoblauch, Rustin & Sorter, 2005), Beebe and Lachmann see 'the mother-infant interactions as a continuous reciprocally coordinated process, co-created moment-to-moment by both partners. Each partner affects the behaviour of the other, often in split seconds (Beebe, 1982; Beebe & Stern, 1977; Stern, 1971), but not necessarily in similar symmetrical or equal ways' (Beebe & Lachmann, 2014, pp. 4–5).

In their recent experimental design into mother-infant interactions, four-month-old infants were filmed with their mothers instructed to play with their infants as they would at home, but without any toys. One camera is focused on the mother's face and hands, and one camera on the infant's face and hands. The two cameras generate a split-screen view, so that both partners can be seen at the same time. The mother and the infant are left alone in the filming chamber to play for five to ten minutes. The researchers then code two and a half minutes of each mother-infant film, second by second, 'a micro-analysis'. It took ten years to obtain the data for this research.

We describe the design of the research project to illustrate the richness of the data obtained. Descriptions of how the mother-infant interacted are outlined in two distinct categories. One category is what is observed in real time by observers of the interaction. The second category of observation is provided by a second-by-second microanalysis of this same section of the film. This process slows down the communication into Stern's 'split second world' (Stern, 1971; Beebe & Stern, 1997). This level of viewing reveals what is lost to the naked eye in real time; it reveals the subtle missteps in the dance. This is a similar methodology to the video analysis used by McCluskey in her research on goal-corrected empathic attunement.

A 'future' secure mother-infant interaction at four months

Beebe and Lachmann give a detailed description of what a future secure mother-infant dyad would look like at four months. The video analysis captured in real time a 'facial mirroring' process between mother and infant. However, when watched using the microanalysis methodology this analysis revealed aspects of the interaction that cannot be discerned in real time. For example:

the complex interaction that occurs around the infant looking down, cannot be discerned in real time. It is a moment of a very slight 'misstep in the dance'. Beebe notes that 'watching in real time my students often insist that the infant looked down because the mother moved her finger in towards the infant's belly, about to poke. But the microanalysis reveals the opposite order: the infant looked down first, the mother reacted with some facial tensing and then lightly poked the infant's belly.

(p. 11)

There is also evidence of a repair of a larger 'misstep in the dance'.

What is seen in the microanalysis that is not visible in the real-time viewing is maternal management of infant distress. The mother achieves this through 'joining' exactly her infant's 'uh-oh' expression.

The infant's eyes are closed during this moment. But we can see that the mother joins the exact quality of the infant's distress, exquisitely sensing the infant's state. This moment is not visible in real time video, but is the key to this interaction. Then both participants participate in the repair.

(p. 14)

This matching is part and parcel of the process of goal-corrected empathic attunement (GCEA). The caregiver attunes to the distress through the use of paraphrasing the exact words used by the careseeker to let them know that the caregiver is on the same wavelength, or by regulating the non-verbal behaviour through affect attunement through the different modalities of tone of voice, posture, eye contact. However, in the successful interactions, where the biological goal of the careseeking system is reached, the caregiver attunes to the state the other is in but does not stay there, returning instead to a state of exploratory caregiving with empathy. This is supporting the careseeker to make the move from the fear aspect of the system for self-defence to the careseeking aspect of the system for self-defence. In this process of interaction the adult careseeker returns to exploratory mode by continuing to explore their affective state, just as the child or infant returns to play or exploration once their careseeking has been assuaged by the interventions of the mother or primary carer.

Recall Fisher's remark about learning to make vocal responses to the client's narrative, which was not only to help the client feel 'met' but to regulate autonomic arousal and keep the frontal cortex online. Beebe and Lachmann make a similar point that:

the patient may be distressed and the therapist may 'enter' the patient's state for a moment by matching or echoing the patient's distressed facial expression with a similar one of her own. Most likely neither partner will be quite aware of this. But it will play an important role in the empathic climate.(p. 14)

A future disorganised mother-infant interaction at four months

Before describing the type of interactions observed in both real time and under their microanalysis, Beebe and Lachmann insert this important proviso that: 'It is important to hold in mind that the mothers of disorganised infants are suffering from unresolved loss, abuse or trauma and are thought to be in a continuing state of fear (Lyons-Ruth et al., 1999; Main & Hess, 1990). In the real-time video, both mother and infant are looking at each other. The infant smiles and whimpers simultaneously (an instance of infant "discrepant affect", positive and negative affect in the same second, which predicts disorganised attachment in our data). The mother smiles (an instance of maternal smile to infant distress, which predicts disorganised attachment in our data). The mother tickles the infant's stomach and asks "are you happy?" (an example of mother not acknowledging the infant's distress). Later in the video it is possible to see the mother displays a "mock surprise" expression to the infant's distress. The infant then simultaneously smiles and whimpers. The infant then immediately brings his hands up to his face, obscuring it with his hands while whimpering' (Beebe & Lachmann, 2014, p. 15).

Notice the level of discordant signals occurring in the interaction. This discordance at the non-verbal level of interaction is predictive of disorganized attachment at twelve months of age. What Beebe and Lachmann's research is empirically demonstrating is 'a process of disturbance as it is being formed. It is laying the foundation of certain expectancies of dysregulation interaction at such an early age'.

Microanalysis of a future disorganised dyad

We only outline in brief some of the interactions observed by the researchers in this microanalysis.

In second 19: the infant is looking down, with strong facial distress, a frown and pre-cry face. The mother has a closed neutral mouth. (She does not acknowledge or mirror her infant's distress, she looks detached.)

In second 19 (change within second): the infant is more upset, whimpering and his frown deepens while his fist is still clenched. The mother grimaces, with a hint of disgust, and moves her head back.

According to Beebe and Lachmann, 'this is a very difficult moment to observe, the level of mismatch is disturbing' (p. 16). The mother does not seem able to respond empathically to the infant's distress. The authors remind us that:

> the mother's own prior history of unresolved distress is triggered by the infant's distress, disturbing her ability to respond empathically. This future dyad is a good example of the 4-month pattern of communication difficulties of dyads on the way to disorganised compared to secure attachment.
>
> (p. 17)

Again, the authors emphasize 'although it is easy to feel for the infant, it is important to have empathy for the mothers as well' (p. 6). This is something with which we agree and developed in the previous chapter on the caregiving self as the keystone system.

Summary of future disorganised (vs. secure) dyads at four months

'In summary, four-month infants who will be classified disorganised (vs. secure) at twelve months were more likely to be male and to show complex forms of emotional dysregulation;

More vocal distress, and more combined facial and/or vocal distress;

More discrepant facial and vocal affect;

Lowered engagement self-contingency, an emotional destabilization;

More failure to touch, less touching one's own skin, and greater likelihood of continuing in a 'no touch' state, all of which compromises infant access to arousal regulation through touch in the context of increased distress'

(Beebe & Lachmann, 2014, pp. 119–120).

Mothers of four-month infants who will be classified disorganised (vs. secure) at twelve months were more likely to show the following patterns:

'Extensive (20% of the time or more) gazing away from infant's face, and less predictable self-contingency patterns of looking at and away from the infant, compromising infant ability to expect and rely on predictable maternal visual attention;

Extensive (20% of the time or more) 'looming' head movements which were relatively unpredictable, interpreted as potentially threatening;

Greater likelihood of positive and/or surprise expressions while infants were distressed, interpreted as maternal emotional 'denial' of infant distress;

Lowered emotional (facial-visual engagement) coordination with infant's ups and downs, interpreted as maternal emotional withdrawal from distressed infants;

Heightened maternal facial self-contingency, an overly stable face leading to a 'closed-up' inscrutable face;

Lowered maternal contingent touch coordination with infant touch, a form of withdrawal.

The two findings of lowered maternal engagement coordination and lowered maternal touch coordination compromise infant interactive efficacy in these domains'

(Beebe & Lachmann, 2014, pp. 119–120).

We take these observations of how the caregiver responds to the careseeker very seriously across the multi modalities of affective communication. Drawing on the data from all the infant-mother observation research, we pay particular attention in the therapeutic space to posture, facial expression, tone of voice, and eye contact respecting the space and distance between the participants in the dyad. This is how our practice has incorporated this data from the research in very practical and meaningful ways. We are aware that as caregivers we are always cuing the other person to come to an open and permeable place inside themselves and not to go into postural collapse as a self-soothing behaviour. Calling the person in front of us into relationship through both verbal and non-verbal means is a continuous process of interaction that is at the heart of our practice in adult psychotherapy. We notice what is novel in the interaction, and we bring the person's attention to what we see without shaming the person. We see what is novel as indicative of a change within the dynamic organization of the attachment dynamics within the person. This can illuminate patterns of communication that are still active in the present but have their origins in very early non-verbal responses from the primary carers in the person's infancy.

In their conclusion, Beebe and Lachmann (2014) note that:

> In considering the relevance of our research on the 4-month origins of attachment to adult treatment, our goal is to view the patient through an adaptive lens rather than a pathological one. The patient attempts to cope with the stress of a developmental trajectory that began with contradictory and conflicted patterns of communication and engagement patterns which at times generated alarm and threat. These patterns disturb the patient's most fundamental processes of knowing the partner, being known by the partner and of knowing herself.
>
> (p. 92)

Beebe and Lachmann note "that there is a striking fit between their findings at four months and those of Lyons-Ruth at twelve to eighteen months, both of whom document maternal failures of recognition in disorganised attachment, and theories of Bromberg (2011) and Benjamin (1995) in adult treatment as well as theories in neurobiology (Schore, 2009, 2011; Siegel, 1999, 2012; Porges et al., 1994. Bromberg, 2011) propose that the developmental trauma of non-recognition is so enormous that it is continually dreaded, like the shadow of a tsunami' (p. 69).

Reading how Beebe and Lachmann (2014) extrapolated their research, we were powerfully struck by the similarity in their findings with those of McCluskey (2005). In her research, McCluskey was able to examine the video playback of the dyadic interaction at the rate of twenty-five frames a second. Like Beebe and Lachmann, this gave her access to what is missed from real-time observation.

> As a first step I needed to see whether the concept of affect attunement, which had been developed in the infant domain (Stern, 1985), fitted the

adult domain, and in ways that it might need developing to meet the needs of the adult context. Having established a definition of the concept I needed to see whether it could be reliably rated.

(McCluskey, 2005, p. 90)

Achieving an independent measure of the process of goal-corrected empathic attunement 'proved to be dependent on moving away from considering individual behaviour to observing the process of interaction'.

We will now look at the signals that McCluskey used in her research to focus on the behaviour of the careseeker and the caregiver in the therapeutic pairs which she used.

I judged the 'state' the careseeker was in primarily through a detailed examination of the audio and video tracks of the video recording. I noted the pitch, tone, and pace of the voice, the facial expression, whether the person made or avoided eye contact, has a centred, slumped (collapsed) or rigid posture and then made rough classifications into low, medium, high, and regulated vitality affects. Using these categories (voice, face, eye, and posture) the profiles of the different vitality states looked as follows:

Low vitality states

The voice is low pitched, the pace of speaking is slow, the facial expression is relatively immobile, there is avoidance of the eye contact when speaking, posture is generally slumped and in general the person seems withdrawn into themselves. The whole face looks rather immobile, though there is some expression around the eyes.

Medium vitality levels

The person expresses themselves similarly to the above but there is more eye contact when speaking, the posture is less withdrawn and slumped and the speech is not as low or slow. There could be a suggestion or hint of a slight rocking motion. The upper part of the face around the eyes seems more expressive in contrast to the muscles in the jaw and around the mouth, which appears tense.

High vitality levels

The person's speech is fast and rapid, there is a lot of intense eye contact, a lot of movement in the body and a tendency to lean into the space between the careseeker and the caregiver. The facial expression looks strained and tense. The general impression is of intensity.

Regulated vitality levels

> The person tends to look 'present' behind their eyes and to look lively and responsive. They make eye contact with the caregiver and tend to have a loosely centred posture. Their facial expression is fluid and mobile and their voice tone has a grounded and resonant tone.
>
> (McCluskey, 2005, p. 195)

See McCluskey's 2005 book 'To Be Met as a Person' for a full description of this research and note in particular the series of photographs produced showing the vitality levels as communicated between a careseeker and a caregiver. McCluskey says:

> I do not think what I am trying to convey could come across as clearly without the visual evidence ... What is dramatic about the photographs is the contrast between those caregivers who are alert and affectively responsive to the careseeker and those who are not. What is also visibly clear is that goal-corrected empathic attuned interaction is accompanied by tension which shows in the face and posture.
>
> (McCluskey, 2005, pp. 195–219)

The most recent research by Beebe and Lachmann is showing us the early mother-infant patterns of communication across the different modes of communication involving attention, affect, orientation, and touch. It provides the empirical evidence from the infant research studies for what McCluskey's (2005) research shows in the adult-to-adult psychotherapy domain.

When these interactions are successful they allow the goals of different goal-corrected biological systems to reach their goal. They support the development of a secure attachment as measured by the Ainsworth et al. (1978) strange situation test. When these interactions do not go well, the systems that are aroused in the careseeker fail to reach their goal and the person remains at the mercy of an unregulated fear system, infiltrating the rest of the systems within the attachment dynamic. The attachment status which is the most dysregulated is the disorganised attachment status as identified by Main and Hess (1990).

The use of video recordings as part of McCluskey's training in goal-corrected empathic attunement and in exploratory goal-corrected psychotherapy plays a vital role in helping professional caregivers of various therapeutic modalities explore these patterns of interaction as part of their training in this particular therapeutic model. This use of video analysis has links to the one-year infant observation training required as part of most psychoanalytic psychotherapy training in the UK and elsewhere.

Conclusion

This chapter charts an overview of how our current practice of exploratory goal-corrected psychotherapy (EGCP) has evolved from its roots in the psychoanalytic object relations tradition, primarily though the work of Fairbairn, the philosophical work of John MacMurray, Ian Suttie, and John Derg Sutherland.

This philosophical, theoretical, and clinical database laid the foundation for Bowlby's work on attachment. Bowlby focused on the observable phenomena of emotional and behavioural responses to separation and loss. He worked closely with the cine photographer James Robertson and his wife Joyce, who captured detailed footage of these phenomena. The findings supported the impact of actual experience on a child's life as opposed to what they fantasized might have happened to them. This departure from classical intrapsychic phenomena to observable behaviour was crucial in bringing together the research data of Ainsworth – and later the work of Stern, Beebe and Lachmann, and many others – with the work of McCluskey in the UK, who worked on translating this template of mother-infant observation studies to the adult-to-adult psychotherapy domain.

It is this consilience between the clinical and the empirical, the mother-infant, and the therapist (caregiver) and patient (careseeker) that is being supported by the neuroscience of today, which includes the work of Schore, Siegel, Porges, Odgen, and others. In making these links between the theoretical, the clinical, and the observable, our practice has emerged and evolved as a usable model for understanding our behaviour from an evolutionary, biological, interpersonal, and relational perspective.

Bowlby stated that he was surprised to find he had started to plough the same field as Freud almost sixty years ago, although he had started out in the corner diametrically opposed to where Freud had started. By continuing to plough this field, we have developed the Bowlby, Heard-Lake-McCluskey developmental line in the adult psychotherapy world. We have developed a practice of individual and group psychotherapy for adults that has a rich heritage and a lineage that goes back to the founders of psychotherapy. As Freud said: 'Everywhere I go I find a poet has been there already.'

References

Agazarian, Y.M. (1997). *Systems-Centered Therapy for Groups.* New York: Guilford.

Ainsworth, M.D.S., Blehar, M.C., Waters, E. and Wall, S. (1978). *Patterns of Attachment: A Psychological Study of the Strange Situation.* Hillsdale, NJ: Erlbaum Associates.

Ainsworth, M.D.S. and Wittig, B.A. (1969). 'Attachment and the exploratory behaviour of one-year-olds in a strange situation.' In B.M. Foss (Ed.), *Determinants of Infant Behaviour Vol 4* (pp. 113–136). London: Methuen.

Ainsworth, M.D.S., Bell, S.M. and Stayton, D. (1974). 'Infant-mother attachment and social development' In M.P. Richards (Ed.), *The Introduction of the Child into a Social World* (pp. 99–135). London: Cambridge University Press.

Balint, M. (1952). *Primary Love and Psycho-Analytic Technique (2nd Ed).* London: Tavistock Publications.

Balint, M. (1968). *The Basic Fault.* London: Tavistock.

Beebe, B. (1982). 'Micro-timing in mother-infant communication.' In M.R. Key (Ed.), *Nonverbal Communication Today.* Series edited by J. Fishman, Contributions to the Sociology of Language, Vol 33. New York: Mouton.

Beebe, B. and Lachmann, F. (2002). *Infant Research and Adult Treatment: Co-constructing Interactions.* Hillsdale, NJ: Analytic Press.

Beebe, B. and Lachmann, F. (2003). The relational turn in psychoanalysis: A dyadic systems view from infant research. *Contemporary Psychoanalysis,* 39(3): pp. 379–409.

Beebe, B. and Lachmann, F. (2014). *The Origins of Attachment Infant Research and Adult Treatment.* New York: Routledge.

Beebe, B. and McCrorie, E. (2010). The optimum midrange: Infant research, literature and romantic attachment. *Attachment: New Directions in Psychotherapy and Relational Psychoanalysis,* 4: pp. 39–58.

Beebe, B. and Stern, D. (1977). 'Engagement-disengagement and early object experiences'. In N. Freedman and S. Grand (Eds.), *Communicative Structures and Psychic Structures* (pp. 35–55). New York: Plenum Press.

Beebe, B., Jaffe, J. and Lachmann, F. (1992). 'A dyadic systems view of communication.' In N. Skolnick and S. Warshaw (Eds.), *Relational Perspectives in Psychoanalysis* (pp. 61–68). Hillsdale, NJ: Analytic Press.

Beebe, B., Knoblauch, S., Rustin, J. and Sorter, D. (2005). *Forms of Intersubjectivity in Infant Research and Adult Treatment.* New York: Other Press.

Beebe, B., Jaffe, J., Markese, S., Buck, K., Chen, H., Cohen, P., Bahrick, L., Andrews, H. and Feldstein, S. (2010). The origins of 12-month attachment: A microanalysis of 4-month mother-infant observation. *Attachment and Human Development*, 12, 1: pp. 3–141.

Benjamin, J. (1995). Like Subjects, Love Objects. New Haven, CT: Yale University Press.

Bird, B. (1972). 'Notes on Transference: Universal Phenomenon and Hardest Part of Analysis'. In R. Langs (Ed.) (1990) *Classics in Psycho-Analytic Technique*. Lanham, MD: Rowman and Littlefield Publishers.

Bollas, C. (1987) *The Shadow of the Object: Psychoanalysis of the Unthought Known*. London: Free Association Books.

Bowlby, J. (1951). *Maternal care and mental health*. World Health Organisation, Monograph Series No. 2.

Bowlby, J. (1957). An ethological approach to research on child development. *British Journal of Medical Psychology*, 30(4): pp. 230–240.

Bowlby, J. (1969). *Attachment and Loss (Vol. 1, Attachment)*. London: Hogarth Press.

Bowlby, J. (1973). *Attachment and Loss (Vol. 2, Separation, Anxiety and Anger)*. London: Hogarth Press; New York: Basic Books.

Bowlby, J. (1974). 'Problems of marrying research with clinical and social needs.' In K. J. Connolly and J. S. Bruner (Eds.), *The Growth of Competence* (pp. 303–307). London and New York: Academic Press.

Bowlby, J. (1978). 'Attachment theory and its therapeutic implications.' In C. Feinstein and P.L. Giovacchini (Eds.), *Adolescent Psychiatry: Developmental and Clinical studies, Vol 6* (pp. 5–33). New York: Jason Aronson.

Bowlby, J. (1979). 'Self-reliance and some conditions that promote it.' In *The Making and Breaking of Affectionate Bonds*. London: Tavistock Publications.

Bowlby, J. (1980). *Attachment and Loss (Vol. 3, Loss, Sadness and Depression)*. London: Hogarth Press. New York: Basic Books.

Bowlby, J. (1988). 'On knowing what you are not supposed to know and feeling what you are not supposed to feel.' In *A Secure Base: Clinical Applications of Attachment Theory* (pp. 99–119). London: Routledge.

Bowlby, J. (1991). The role of the psychotherapist's personal resources in the therapeutic situation. *Tavistock Gazette* (Autumn).

Brazelton, T.B. and Cramer, B.G. (1990). *The Earliest Relationship*. Reading, UK: Addison-Wesley.

Bromberg, P. (2011). *The Shadow of the Tsunami and the Growth of the Relational Mind*. London and New York: Routledge.

Bromberg, P.M. (1998). *Standing in the Spaces: Essays on clinical process, trauma, and dissociation*. Hillsdale, NJ: Analytic Press.

Bucci, W. (2005). The interplay of sub symbolic and symbolic processes in psychoanalytic treatment: Commentary on paper by Steven H. Knoblauch. *Psychoanalytic Dialogue*, 15: pp. 873–885.

Casement, P. (1982). Some pressures on the analyst for physical contact during the reliving of an early trauma. *International Review of Psycho-Analysis* 9: pp. 279–286.

Casement, P. (2002). *Learning From Our Mistakes: Beyond Dogma in Psychoanalysis and Psychotherapy*. London: Brunner-Routledge.

Casement, P. (2014). *On Learning from the Patient*. London: Routledge.

Cassidy, J. (1988). Child-mother attachment and the self in six-year-olds. *Child Development*, 59: pp. 121–134.

Cassidy, J. and Shaver, P.R. (Eds.) (1999). *Handbook of Attachment*. New York: Guilford Press.

Chused, J.F. (1998). 'The evocative power of enactments.' In S.J. Ellman and M. Moskowitz (Eds.), *Enactment: Toward a New Approach to the Therapeutic Relationship* (pp. 93–109). Northvale, NJ: Jason Aronson.

Chused, R.H. (1986). Married women's property and inheritance by widows in Massachusetts: A Study of Wills Probated Between 1800 and 1850. *Berkeley Women's Law Journal*, 42.

Clarke, G. (2003). Personal relations theory: Suttie, Fairbairn, Macmurray and Sutherland. Paper presented at the Legacy of Fairbairn and Sutherland Conference. International Psychotherapy Institute and Scottish Institute of Human Relations, Edinburgh.

Clarke, G. (2005). 'Personal relations theory: Suttie, Fairbairn, Macmurray and Sutherland.' In D. Scharff and J. Scharff (Eds.), *The Legacy of Fairbairn and Sutherland, Psychotherapeutic Applications*. London and New York: Routledge.

Coltart, N. (1996/2003). *The Baby and the Bathwater*. London: Karnac.

Crittenden, P.M. (1995). 'Attachment and Psychopathology.' In S. Goldberg, R. Muir and J. Kerr (Eds.), *Attachment Theory: Social, Developmental and Clinical Perspectives*. London: The Analytic Press.

Damasio, A. (1994). *Decartes' Error: Emotion, reason and the human brain*. New York: Putnam.

Damasio, A. (2000). *The Feeling of What Happens: Body, Emotion and the Making of Consciousness*. London: Vintage.

Damasio, A. (2018). *The Strange Order of Things: Life, Feeling, and the Making of Cultures*. New York: Pantheon Books.

Decety, J. and Lamm, C. (2009). 'Empathy versus Personal Distress: Recent Evidence from Social Neuroscience'. In J. Decety and W. Ickes (Eds.), *The Social Neuroscience of Empathy* (pp. 199–214). Cambridge, UK: MIT Press.

Department for Education (2008). Haringey Local Safeguarding Children Board. Serious Case Review 'Child A'. Published by the UK Department for Education on 26 October, 2010.

Department of Health (2004). The Government Response to the Recommendations and Conclusions of the Health Select Committee's Inquiry into Elder Abuse. London: HMSO.

De Wolff, M.S. and Van IJzendoorn, M.H. (1997). Sensitivity and attachment. A meta-analysis on parental antecedents of infant attachment. *Child Development*, 68: pp. 571–591.

Downes, C. and McCluskey, U. (1985). Sharing expertise and responsibility for learning on a postgraduate qualifying course in social work. *Journal of Social Work Practice*, 2: pp. 24–40.

Eger, E. (2017). *The Choice*. New York: Scribner.

Emde, R.N. (1983). The prerepresentational self and its affective core. *The Psychoanalytic Study of the Child*, 38: pp. 165–192.

Emde, R.N. (1985). An adaptive view of infants' emotions: Functions for self and knowing. *Social Sciences Information*, 24: pp. 237–341.

Epstein, O.B. (2015). Letter to John Bowlby, editorial in *Attachment: New Directions in Psychotherapy and Relational Psychoanalysis*, 9(3) November.

Epstein, O.B. (2017). The Occupied Body: On Chronic Fatigue, Co-regulation and Psychoneuroimmunology (PNI). *Attachment: New Directions in Psychotherapy and Relational Psychoanalysis, A Special Issue Dedicated to the Theme of Pain*, 11(3) December.

Esquerro, A. (2017). *Encounters with John Bowlby. Tales of Attachment*. London and New York: Routledge.

Fairbairn, W.R.D. (1940). Schizoid factors in the personality. In *Psychoanalytic Studies of the Personality* (pp. 3–27). London: Tavistock.

Fairbairn, W.R.D. (1941). A Revised Psychopathology of the Psychoses and Psychoneurosis. In *Psychoanalytic Studies of the Personality* (pp. 28–58). London: Tavistock.

Fairbairn, W.R.D. (1952). *Psychoanalytic studies of the personality*. London: Tavistock.

Fairbairn, W.R.D. (1994). 'Synopsis of an Object Relations Theory of the Personality.' In J.S. Goldstein and D.B. Rinsley (Eds.), *Fairbairn and the Origins of Object*. London: Free Association Books.

Fisher, J. (2017). Twenty-Five Years of Trauma Treatment: What have we learned? *Attachment: New Directions in Psychotherapy and Relational Psychoanalysis*, 11(3).

Fonagy, P., Moran, G.S., Steele, M. and Steele, H. (1992). 'The integration of psychoanalytic theory and work on attachment: The issues of intergenerational psychic processes'. In D. Stern and M. Ammaniti (Eds.), *Attacmento E Psiconalis* (pp. 19–30). Bari, Italy: Laterza.

Fonagy, P., Steele, M. and Steele, H. (1991). Maternal representations of attachment during pregnancy predicts the organisation of infant-mother attachment at one year of age. *Child Development*, 62: pp. 880–893.

Freud, S. (1914). 'Remembering, repeating and working-through (further recommendations on the technique of psychoanalysis)'. *Standard Edition 12*: pp. 145–156.

Gergely, G. (1992). Developmental Reconstructions: Infancy from the point of view of psychoanalysis and developmental psychology. *Psychoanalysis and Contemporary Thought*, 15: pp. 3–55.

Gergely, G. and Fonagy, P. (1998). States of mind. Paper presented at the International Attachment Network series of seminars on intersubjectivity, London.

Gergely, G. and Watson, J.S. (1996). The social biofeedback theory of parental affect-mirroring: The development of emotional self-awareness and self-control in infancy. *International Journal of Psycho-Analysis*, 77: pp. 1181–1212.

Ginot, E. (2007). Intersubjectivity and neuroscience: Understanding enactments and their therapeutic significance within emerging paradigms. *Psychoanalytic Psychology*, 24, No. 2: pp. 317–332.

Goffman, E. (1961). *Asylums: Essays on the social situation of mental patient and other inmates*. New York: Anchor Books.

Gomez, L. (1997). *An Introduction to Object Relations*. London: Free Association Books.

Grossman, K., Fremmer-Bombik, E., Rudolph, J. and Grossmann, K.E. (1988). 'Maternal attachment representations as related to child-mother attachment patterns and maternal sensitivity and acceptance of her infant'. In R.A. Hinde and J. Stevenson-Hinde (Eds.), *Relations within Families*. Oxford, UK: Oxford University Press.

Grossmann, K., Grossmann, K.E., Spangler, G., Suess, G. and Unzner, L. (1985). 'Maternal sensitivity and newborns' orientation responses as related to quality of attachment in northern Germany.' In I. Bretherton and E. Waters (Eds.), *Growing points in attachment theory and research monographs of the Society for Research in Child Development*, 50: pp. 233–278.

Grotstein, J.S. and Rinsley, D.B. (Eds.) (1994). *Fairbairn and the Origins of Object Relations*. New York/London: The Guilford Press.

Guntrip, H. (1961). *Personality Structure and Human Interaction*. London: The Hogarth Press.

Guntrip, H. (1968). *Schizoid Phenomena, Object Relations and the Self*. London: The Hogarth Press.

Guntrip, H. (1975) My experience of analysis with Fairbairn and Winnicott. *International Review of Psychoanalysis*, 2: pp. 145–156.

Haldane, J.D. and McCluskey, U. (1977). Parents and Teenagers: Development in War and Peace. *Irish Journal of Sociology*, 5, 3/4.

Haldane, J.D., and McCluskey, U. (1980a) Working with Couples and Families: Experience of training, consultation and supervision. *Journal of Family Therapy*, 2: pp. 163–179.

Haldane, J.D. and McCluskey, U. (1980b). Working with Couples and Families: A note on some issues for research. *Association of Family Therapy Newsletter*.

Haldane, J.D., and McCluskey, U. (1982). Existentialism and Family Therapy: A Neglected Perspective. *Journal of Family Therapy*, 4: pp. 117–132.

Haldane, J.D. and McCluskey, U. (1993). 'Therapy with Couples and Families.' In R.E. Kendell and A.K. Zealley (Eds.), *Companion to Psychiatric Studies (5th Ed)* (pp. 891–913). London: Churchill Livingstone.

Haldane, J.D., McCluskey, U. and Clarke, D. (1986). Does Marriage Matter? A perspective and model for action. *Journal of Social Work Practice*, 2: pp. 31–45.

Haldane, J.D., McCluskey, U. and Peacey, M. (1980). A residential facility for families in Scotland: Developments in prospect and retrospect. *International Journal of Family Psychiatry*, 1: pp. 357–372.

Hazell, J. (2000). 'An Object Relations Perspective on the Development of the Person.' In U. McCluskey and C.A. Hooper (Eds.), *Psychodynamic Perspectives on Abuse: The Cost of Fear* (pp. 25–39). London and Philadelphia: Jessica Kingsley.

Heaney, S. (1995). The Redress of Poetry. New York: Faber and Faber.

Heard, D. (1978). From object relations to attachment theory. *British Journal of Medical Psychology*, 51: pp. 67–76.

Heard, D. (1982). Family systems and the attachment dynamic. *Journal of Family Therapy*, 4: pp. 99–116.

Heard, D. (1988). 'Introduction: historical perspective.' In I. Suttie, *The Origins of Love and Hate*. London: Free Association Books.

Heard, D. and Lake, B. (1986). The attachment dynamic in adult life. *British Journal of Psychiatry*, 149: pp. 430–438.

Heard, D. and Lake, B. (1997). *The Challenge of Attachment for Caregiving*. London: Karnac.

Heard, D., Lake, B. and McCluskey, U. (2009/12). *Attachment Therapy with Adolescents and Adults: Theory and Practice Post-Bowlby*. London: Karnac.

Hofer, M.A. (1983). 'On the relationship between attachment and separation processes in infancy.' In R. Plutchik and H. Kellerman (Eds.), *Emotion, Theory, Research and Experience, 2* (pp. 199–219). New York and London: Academic Press.

Holmes, J. (2009). 'Getting it Together: From Attachment Research to Clinical Practice'. In J. Obegi and E. Berant (Eds.), *Attachment Theory and Research in Clinical Work with Adults* (pp. 490–514). New York: Guilford.

Holmes, J. (2010). *Exploring in security towards an attachment-informed psychoanalytic psychotherapy*. London and New York: Routledge.

Humphries, S. (1998). TV programme: *'Sex in a cold climate.'* Directed by Steve Humphries, Testimony Films, Channel 4 Television Corporation. Available at: www.vimeo.com/13158888

Hunter, V. (2015). John Bowlby: An Interview by Virginia Hunter. *Attachment: New Directions in Psychotherapy and Relational Psychoanalysis*, 9, July: pp. 138–157.

Independent Inquiry into Child Sexual Abuse (2015). Independent inquiry into child sexual abuse. Available at https://childsexualabuseinquiry.independent.gov.uk/

Jaffe, J., Beebe, B., Feldstein, S., Crown, C. and Jasnow, M. (2001). Rhythms of dialogue in infancy. *Monographs of the Society for Research in Child Development*, 66(2), Serial No. 264: pp. 1–132.

James, H. (1881). *The Portrait of a Lady*. Boston, MA: Houghton, Mifflin and Company.

Khan, M. (1974). *The Privacy of the Self: Papers on Psychoanalytic Theory and Technique*. New York: International Universities Press.

Khan, M. (1979). *Alienation in perversions*. London: Karnac.

Kiersky, S. and Beebe, B. (1994). The reconstruction of early nonverbal relatedness in the treatment of difficult patients: A special form of empathy. *Psychoanalytic Dialogues*, 4(3): pp. 389–408.

Kirkwood, C. (2005). 'The persons-in-relation perspective: Sources and synthesis.' In D. Scharff and J. Scharff (Eds.), *The Legacy of Fairbairn and Sutherland, Psychotherapeutic Applications*. London and New York: Routledge.

Lake, B. (1985). Concept of ego strength in psychotherapy. *British Journal of Psychiatry*, 147: pp. 471–478.

LeDoux, J. (1998). *The Emotional Brain*. London: Weidenfeld and Nicolson.

LeDoux, J. (2012). Rethinking the Emotional Brain. *Neuron*, 73, Issue 5: p. 1052.

Lentil, L. (1995). Film: Dear Daughter. Directed by Louis Lentil. Available from Crescendo Concepts, Dublin. http://www.iftn.ie/filmography/?act1=recordandaid= 70andrid1853andsr=1andonly=1andhl=dear+daughterandtpl=filmography_dets

Lintern, S. (2012). *Health Service Journal*, 22 (November).

Lost Innocents (2001). Righting the record – Report on child migration. Commonwealth of Australia. Available at: www.aph.gov.au

Luyten, P. and De Meulemeester, C. (2017). Understanding and Treatment of Patients with Persistent Somatic Complaints. *Attachment: New Directions in Psychotherapy and Relational Psychoanalysis, A Special Issues Dedicated to the Theme of Pain*, 11(3) December.

Lyons-Ruth, K. (1999). The two-person unconscious. *Psychoanalytic Inquiry*, 19: pp. 576–617.

Lyons-Ruth, K. and Block, D. (1996). The disturbed caregiving system. Relations among childhood trauma, maternal caregiving, and infant affect and attachment. *Infant Mental Health Journal*, 17(3): pp. 257–275.

Lyons-Ruth, K., Bronfman, E. and Parson, E. (1999). Maternal disrupted affective communication, maternal frightened or frightening behaviour and disorganised infant attachment strategies. *Monographs of the Society for Research in Child Development*, 64(3), Serial No. 258.

Lyons-Ruth, K., Yellin, C., Melnick, S. and Atwood, G. (2005). Expanding the concept of unresolved mental states: Hostile/helpless states of mind on the adult attachment interview are associated with disrupted mother-infant communication and infant disorganisation. *Development and Psychopathology*, 17: pp. 1–23.

Maclean, P.D. (1990). *The Triune Brain in Evolution*. New York: Plenum Press.

Macmurray, J. (1961). *Persons in Relation*. London: Faber and Faber.

McCluskey, U. (1983). Teddy Bears: Facilitators of love, friendship and therapy. *Journal of Social Work Practice*, 1: pp. 14–35.

McCluskey, U. (1987). 'In praise of feeling, the ethics of intervention.' In S. Walrond-Skinner and D. Watson (Eds.), *The Ethics of Family Therapy* (pp. 56–71): London and New York: Routledge and Kegan Paul.

McCluskey, U. (1990). Money in marriage. *Journal of Social Work Practice*, IV: pp. 16–30.

McCluskey, U. (2000). 'Abuse in religious institutions.' In U. McCluskey and C.A. Hooper (Eds.), *The Psychodynamic Perspectives on Abuse. The Cost of Fear* (pp. 100–117). London: Jessica Kingsley.

McCluskey, U. (2001). *A Theory of Caregiving in Adult Life. Developing and Measuring the Concept of Goal Corrected Empathic Attunement, Vol. 1 and 2*. York, UK: University of York Library.

McCluskey, U. (2002). 'The Dynamics of Attachment and Systems-Centred Group Psychotherapy: The communication, regulation and exploration of affective states.' In J. Savege Scharff and D.E. Scharff (Eds.), *The Legacy of Fairbairn and Sutherland*. London: Routledge.

McCluskey, U. (2003). 'Theme focused family therapy: Working with the dynamics of emotional abuse and neglect within an attachment and systems perspective.' In M. Bell and K. Wilson (Eds.), *The Practitioner's Guide to Working with Families*. London: Macmillan.

McCluskey, U. (2005). *To be Met as a Person: The dynamics of attachment in professional encounters*. London and New York: Karnac.

McCluskey, U. (2007a). 'Attachment therapy with couples, affect regulation and dys-regulation in couple relationships: Effective and ineffective responses to painful states by therapists and partners.' In M. Ludlam and V. Nyberg (Eds.), *Couples Attachments: Theoretical and Clinical Studies*. London: Karnac.

McCluskey, U. (2007b). A model of group psychotherapy based on extended attachment theory: A preliminary report. *Inside Out. The Journal of the Irish Association of Humanistic and Integrative Psychotherapy*, 52: pp. 71–81.

McCluskey, U. (2008). Attachment-based therapy in groups: Exploring a new theoretical paradigm with professional caregivers. *Attachment: New Directions in Psychotherapy and Relational Psychoanalysis*, 2(2): pp. 204–215.

McCluskey, U. (2010). Understanding the self and understanding therapy: An attachment perspective. *Context*, February: pp. 29–32.

McCluskey, U. (2011a). Reflections on my journey as a family therapist in Scotland and North Yorkshire in the 1970s and the 1980s. *Context*, July: pp. 55–57.

McCluskey, U. (2011b). The therapist as a fear-free caregiver supporting change in the dynamic organisation of the self. *Association of University and College Counselling*, May: pp. 12–18.

McCluskey, U. and Bingley Miller, L. (1995). Theme focused family therapy: The inner emotional world of the family. *Journal of Family Therapy*, 17: pp. 411–434.

McCluskey, U. and Duerden, S. (1993). Pre-verbal communication: The role of play in establishing rhythms of communication between self and other. *Journal of Social Work Practice*, 7: pp. 17–29.

McCluskey, U. and Gunn, J. (2015). The dynamics of caregiving: Why are professional caregivers vulnerable to anxiety and burnout, and how do we support their well-being? *Attachment: New Directions in Psychotherapy and Relational Psychoanalysis*, 9(2), July: pp 188–200.

McCluskey, U. and Hooper, C.A. (Eds.) (2000). *Psychodynamic Perspectives on Abuse: The Cost of Fear*. London: Jessica Kingsley.

McCluskey, U., Hooper, C.A. and Bingley Miller, L. (1999). Goal corrected empathic attunement: Developing and rating the concept within an attachment perspective. *Psychotherapy: Theory/Research, Training and Practice*: pp. 80–90.

McCluskey, U., Roger, D. and Nash, P. (1997). A preliminary study of the role of affect attunement in adult psychotherapy. *Journal of Human Relations*, 50: pp. 1261–1275.

McDonald, H. (2013). Ireland apologises for 'slave labour' at Magdalene Laundries. Available at: www.guardian.co.uk/world/2013/fb/19/ireland-apologises-slavelabour-magdalene-laundries

McDougall, J. (1985). *Theatres of the mind: Illusion and truth on the psychoanalytic stage*. London: Free Association Books.

McDougall, J. (1989). *Theatres of the body: A psychoanalytical approach to psychosomatic illness*. London: Free Association Books.

Main, M. (1991). 'Metacognitive knowledge, metacognitive monitoring, and singular (coherent) vs. multiple (incoherent). Model of attachment: Findings and directions for future research.' In C.M. Parkes, J. Stevenson-Hinde and P. Marris (Eds.), *Attachment across the life cycle* (pp. 127–159). London: Routledge.

Main, M. (1995). 'Recent studies in attachment: Overview, with selected implications for clinical work.' In S. Goldberg, R. Muir and J. Kerr (Eds.), *Attachment Theory: Social, Developmental and Clinical Perspectives* (pp. 407–474). London: The Analytic Press.

Main, M. and Cassidy, J. (1988). Categories of response to reunion with the parent at age six: Predicted from attachment classifications and stable over a one-month period. *Developmental Psychology*, 24: pp. 415–426.

Main, M. and Hesse, E. (1990). 'Parents' unresolved traumatic experiences are related to infant disorganised attachment status. Is frightened and/or frightening parental behaviour the linking mechanism'? In M. Greenberg, D. Cicchetti and E. Cummings (Eds.), *Attachment in the preschool years: Theory, research, and intervention* (pp. 161–182). Chicago, IL: University of Chicago Press.

Meltzoff, A.N. (1999). 'Persons and representations: Why infant imitation is important for theories of human development.' In J. Nadel and G. Butterworth (Eds.), *Imitation in Infancy* (pp. 9–35). Cambridge, UK: Cambridge University Press.

Meltzoff, A.N. and Moore, M.K. (1977). Imitation of facial and manual gestures by human neonates. *Science*, 198(4312): pp. 75–78.

Meltzoff, A.N. and Moore, M.K. (1983). Newborn infants imitate adult facial gestures. *Child Development*, 54: pp. 702–709.

Menzies, I.E.P. (1960). A case study in the functioning of social systems as a defence against anxiety: A report on a study of the nursing service of a general hospital. *Human Relations*, 13(2): pp. 439–462.

Mitchell, S. (2009). *Murphy Report*. Report of the omission of investigation into the Catholic Archdiocese of Dublin. Accessed 29 June, 2013. Available at: www.justice.ie./en/JELR/Pages/PB

Murray, L. (1998). 'Contributions of experimental and clinical perturbations of mother-infant communications to the understanding of infant intersubjectivity.' In S. Braten (Ed.), *Intersubjectivity, Communication and Early Ontogeny* (pp. 127–144). Cambridge, UK: Cambridge University Press.

Murray, L. and Trevarthen, C. (1985). 'Emotional regulation of interactions between two-month-olds and their mothers'. In T.M. Field and N.A. Fox (Eds.), *Social Perception in Infants*. Norwood, NJ: Ablex.

Murray, L. and Trevarthen, C. (1986). The infants' role in mother-infant communications. *Journal of Child Language*, 13: pp. 15–29.

Neath, N. and McCluskey, U. (2019). *To be Met as a Person at Work: The effects of early attachment experiences on work relationships*. London: Routledge.

Ogden, P., Minton, K. and Pain, C. (2006). *Trauma and the body A sensorimotor approach to psychotherapy*. London: Norton.

O'Toole, M. (2015). The phenomenon of silence in psychotherapy. *Attachment: New Directions in Psychotherapy and Relational Psychoanalysis*, 9(3), November: pp. 342–360.

O'Toole, M. (2016). A combined approach to psychotherapy, individual and group, from an attachment perspective. *Attachment: New Directions in Psychotherapy and Relational Psychoanalysis*, 10(2), October: pp. 110–131.

O'Toole, M. (2019). The impact of cultural factors on attachment dynamics: A view from Irish society. *Attachment: New Directions in Psychotherapy and Relational Psychoanalysis*, 13(2), November.

Panksepp, J. (1998). *Affective neuroscience: The foundation of human and animal emotions*. New York: Oxford University Press.

Papousek, M. (1994). Melodies in care-givers' speech: A species-specific guidance towards language. *Early Development and Parenting*, 3: pp. 5–17.

Papousek, H. and Papousek, M. (1979). 'Early ontogeny of human social interaction: Its biological roots and social dimensions'. In M.V. Cranach (Ed.), *Human Ethology*. Cambridge, UK: Cambridge University Press.

Perls, F.S., Hefferline, R. and Goodman, P. (1951). *Gestalt therapy. Excitement and growth in the human personality*. New York: Julian Press.

Polster, E. and Polster, M. (1973). *Gestalt Therapy Integrated: Contours of Theory and Practice*. New York: Vintage Books.

Porges, S.W. (2001). The polyvagal theory: Phylogenetic substrates of a social nervous system. *International Journal of Psychophysiology*, 32: pp. 301–318.

Porges, S.W. (2004). Neuroception: A subconscious system for detecting threats and safety. *Zero to Three (J)*, 24(5): pp. 19–24.

Porges, S.W. (2007). The polyvagal perspective. *Biological Psychology*, 74: pp. 116–143.

Porges, S.W. (2011). *Norton Series on Interpersonal Neurobiology. The polyvagal theory, neurophysiological foundations of emotions, attachment, communication and self-regulation*. New York: Norton.

Porges, S.W., Doussard-Roosevelt, J.A. and Maiti, A.K. (1994). Vagal tone and the physiological regulation of emotion. *Monographs of the Society for Research in Child Development*, 59: pp. 167–186.

Raftery, M. (1994). States of Fear. Produced by Mary Raftery for Radio Telefís Eirea (RTE). Accessed 27 April, 2013. Available at: www.imdb.com/title/tt0281225/combined

Refugee Council (2013). Accessed 23 April, 2013. Available at: www.refugeecouncil.org.uk/assets/0002/7295/influecing_Parliment.pdf

Renn, P. (2012). *The Silent Past and the Invisible Present: Memory, Trauma, and Representation in Psychotherapy*. London: Routledge.

Rogers, C.R. (1980). *A Way of Being*. New York: Houghton Mifflin Company.

Rogers, C.R. (2004 [1961]). *On Becoming a Person. A Therapist's View of Psychotherapy*. London: Constable and Company.

Rutter, M. (1981). *Maternal deprivation reassessed (2nd Ed.)*. Harmondsworth, UK: Penguin.

Rutter, M. (1997). 'Clinical implications of attachment concepts. Retrospective and prospective.' In L. Atkinson and K.J. Zucker (Eds.), *Attachment psychopathology* (pp. 17–46). New York: Guilford Press.

Scharff, D.E. (1992). *Refinding the Object and Reclaiming the Self*. Northvale, NJ: Jason Aronson.

Scharff, D.E. and Birtles, E.F. (1994). In *Fairbairn* (1952, [1990]) *Psychoanalytic Studies of the Personality*. London: Routledge.

Scharff, J.S. (2004). 'The British Object Relations Theorists: Fairbairn, Winnicott, Balint, Guntrip, Sutherland, and Bowlby.' In M. Bergmann (Ed.), *Understanding Dissidence and Controversy in the History of Psychoanalysis* (pp. 175–200). New York: Other Press.

Schore, A. (1994). *Affect Regulation and the Origin of the Self: The Neurobiology of Emotional Development*. Hillsdale, NJ: Lawrence Erlbaum Associates.

Schore, A. (2000a). 'Foreword' to the reissue of *Attachment and Loss, Volume 1: Attachment* by John Bowlby. New York: Basic Books.

Schore, A. (2000b). Attachment and the regulation of the right brain. *Attachment & Human Development*, 2: pp. 23–47.

Schore, A. (2001). The effects of relational trauma on right brain development, affect regulation and infant mental health. *Infant Mental Health Journal*, 22: pp. 201–269.

Schore, A. (2002). Dysregulation of the Right Brain: A fundamental mechanism of traumatic attachment and the psychogenesis of post-traumatic stress disorder. *Australian and New Zealand Journal of Psychiatry*, 36(1).

Schore, A. (2003a). 'The seventh annual John Bowlby memorial lecture. Minds in the making: Attachment, the self-organizing brain, and developmentally oriented psychoanalytic psychotherapy.' In J. Corrigall and H. Wilkinson (Eds.), *Revolutionary Connections: Psychotherapy and Neuroscience*. London: Karnac.

Schore, A. (2003b). *Affect Regulation and the Repair of the Self*. New York: W.W. Norton.

Schore, A. (2003c). *Affect Dysregulation and Disorders of the Self*. New York: W.W. Norton.

Schore, A. (2009). 'Attachment trauma and the developing brain: Origins of pathological dissociation'. In P. Dell and J. O'Neil (Eds.), *Dissociation and the dissociative disorders* (pp. 107–131). New York: Routledge.

Schore, A. (2011). 'Preface'. In P. Bromberg (Ed), *The shadow of the tsunami and the growth of the relational mind* (pp. ix–xxxvi). New York: Routledge.

Schore, A. (2012). *The Science of the Art of Psychotherapy*. New York: W.W. Norton.

Siegel, D. (1999). *The developing mind: Towards a neurobiology of interpersonal experience*. New York: Guilford.

Siegel, D. (2003). 'An interpersonal neurobiology of psychotherapy: The developing mind and the resolution of trauma.' In M. Solomon and D. Siegel (Eds.), *Healing Trauma: Attachment, mind, body and brain* (pp. 1–56). New York: Norton.

Siegel, D. (2012). *Pocket guide to interpersonal neurobiology*. New York: Norton.

Sinclair, I. and McCluskey, U. (1996). Invasive partners: An exploration of attachment, communication and family patterns. *Journal of Family Therapy*, 18: pp. 61–79.

Slade, A. (1999). 'The implications of attachment theory and research for adult psychotherapy: Research and clinical perspectives.' In J. Cassidy and P. Shaver (Eds.), *Handbook of Attachment: Theory, research, and clinical applications (2nd Ed)* (pp. 762–782). New York: Guilford.

Slade, A. (2013). 'The place of fear in attachment theory and psychoanalysis: The fifteenth John Bowlby memorial lecture.' In J. Yellin and O.B. Epstein (Eds.), *Terror within and without attachment and disintegration: Clinical work on the edge.* London: Karnac.

Solomon, J. and George, C. (Eds.) (1999). *Attachment Disorganisation.* New York: Guilford Press.

Solomon, M. and Siegel, D.J. (Eds.) (2003). *Healing trauma attachment, mind, body, and brain.* New York: W.W. Norton.

Sonntag, M.E. (2006). I have a lower class body. *Psychoanalytic Dialogues,* 16: pp. 317–331.

Stern, D. (1971). A microanalysis of the mother-infant interaction. *Journal of the American Academy of Child Psychiatry,* 10: pp. 501–507.

Stern, D. (1977). *The first relationship.* Cambridge, MA: Harvard University Press.

Stern, D. (1985). *The Interpersonal World of the Infant: A view from psychoanalysis and developmental psychology.* London: Karnac.

Stern, D. (2000). 'Introduction to the paperback edition'. In D. Stern, *The interpersonal world of the infant: A view from psychoanalysis and developmental psychology.* New York: Basic Books.

Stern, D. (2004). *The Present Moment in Psychotherapy and Everyday Life.* New York: W. W Norton.

Sutherland, J.D. (1989). *Fairbairn's Journey into the Interior.* London: Free Association Books.

Sutherland, J.D. (1993). The autonomous self. *Bulletin of the Menninger Clinic,* 57(1): pp. 3–32.

Suttie, I.D. (1935/88). *The Origins of Love and Hate.* London: Free Association Books.

Symington, N. (1986). *The Analytic Experience: Lectures from the Tavistock.* London: Tavistock Publications.

The Commission to Inquire into Child Abuse Report (20 May, 2009). Government Publications, Co Mayo, Ireland. Accessed 29 June, 2013. Available at: www.childa busecommission.ie /publications/index.html

The Stolen Children Inquiry (1997). *Bringing them Home.* Commonwealth of Australia.

Trevarthen, C. (2016). Pre-birth to three: Professor Colwyn Trevarthen – musicality of language. Available at: https://www.youtube.com/watch?reload=9&v=HL1_tB60hqM

Trevarthen, C. and Hubley, P. (1978). 'Secondary intersubjectivity: Confidence, confiders and acts of meaning in the first year'. In A. Lock (Ed.), *Action, Gesture, and Symbol.* New York: Cambridge University Press.

Tronick, E.Z. (1989). Emotions and Emotional Communication in Infants. *American Psychologist,* 44: pp. 112–119.

Tronick, E.Z. and Cohn, J. (1989). Infant-mother face to face interaction. Age and gender differences in coordination and miscoordination. *Child Development,* 59: pp. 85–92.

Van IJzendoorn, M.H. and De Wolff, M.S. (1997). In search of the absent father. Meta-analysis of infant-father attachment. A rejoinder to our discussants. *Child Development,* 68: pp. 604–609.

Vas Dias, S. (2000). 'Inner Silence: One of the impacts of emotional abuse upon the developing self'. In U. McCluskey and C.A. Hooper (Eds.), *Psychodynamics Perspectives on Abuse: The Cost of Fear* (pp. 159–171). London and Philadelphia: Jessica Kingsley.

Whitaker, D.S. (2000). *Using Groups to Help People.* London: Routledge.

Whitaker, D.S. and Lieberman, M.A. (1964). *Psychotherapy through the group process.* Oxford, UK: Atherton Press.

Wilkinson, M. (2010). *Changing minds in therapy: Emotion, attachment, trauma and neurobiology.* London: Norton.

Winnicott, D.W. (1958). *Collected papers through paediatrics to psycho-analysis.* London: Hogarth Press and the Institute of Psycho-Analysis.

Winnicott, D.W. (1960). 'The Theory of the Parent-Infant Relationship'. In *The Maturational Processes and the Facilitating Environment.* London: Karnac.

Winnicott, D.W. (1965). *The Maturational Processes and the Facilitating Environment.* London: Hogarth.

Winnicott, D.W. (1971a). *Playing and Reality.* London: Tavistock.

Winnicott, D.W. (1971b). *Therapeutic Consultations in Child Psychiatry.* London: Hogarth Press and the Institute of Psycho-Analysis.

Winnicott, D.W. (1974). Fear of Breakdown. *International Review of Psycho-Analysis,* 1: pp. 103–107.

Yontef, G.M. (1988). *Awareness Dialogue and Process Essays on Gestalt Therapy.* New York: The Gestalt Journal Press.

Index